Theories, Practices and Examples for Community and Social Informatics

Theories, Practices and Examples for Community and Social Informatics

Edited by Tom Denison, Mauro Sarrica
and Larry Stillman

Monash University Publishing
Building 4, Monash University
Clayton, Victoria 3800, Australia
www.publishing.monash.edu

Monash University Publishing brings to the world publications which advance the best
traditions of humane and enlightened thought.

Monash University Publishing titles pass through a rigorous process of independent peer
review.

www.publishing.monash.edu/books/tpecsi-9781921867620.html

Series: Social Informatics

Design: Les Thomas

National Library of Australia Cataloguing-in-Publication entry:

Author:	Denison, Tom, editor.
Title:	Theories, practices and examples for community and social informatics / Tom Denison, Mauro Sarrica, and Larry Stillman (editors).
ISBN:	9781921867620 (paperback)
Series:	Social Informatics
Notes:	Includes index.
Subjects:	Community information services.
	Communication in community development.
	Information technology--Social aspects.
	Computer networks--Social aspects.
	Social epistemology.
Dewey Number:	302.2

Printed in Australia by Griffin Press an Accredited ISO AS/NZS 14001:2004
Environmental Management System printer.

The paper this book is printed on is certified against the Forest
Stewardship Council ® Standards. Griffin Press holds FSC chain
of custody certification SGS-COC-005088. FSC promotes
environmentally responsible, socially beneficial and economically viable
management of the world's forests.

FSC
www.fsc.org
MIX
Paper from
responsible sources
FSC® C009448

CONTENTS

CONTRIBUTORS

FRANCESCA COMUNELLO is Assistant Professor at the Department of Communication and Social Research, Sapienza University of Rome (Italy), where she teaches Internet studies. Her research focuses on the intersections between digital technology and society, with a focus on social media. Her work has been presented at national and international conferences. She has authored two books and several articles and book chapters; she has edited or co-edited three books (among them, *Networked Sociability and Individualism*).

ALBERTA CONTARELLO is Professor of Social Psychology at the University of Padova (Italy). Her fields of teaching and research are Social Psychology and Qualitative Methods in Social Psychological Research. Theoretically, she has adopted a social constructivist stance which takes into account psychological processes and places particular emphasis on membership, praxis and value endorsement. Her current interests concern the social construction of knowledge, with particular regard to social issues in phases of change and debate. The macro-level theme is social inclusion vs. exclusion, while specific themes regard ageing, science and gender, ICTs, environmental conflicts and social wellbeing.

TOM DENISON PhD is a Lecturer and Research Associate with the Centre for Organisational and Social Informatics (COSI) in the Faculty of Information Technology at Monash University. He conducts research within the fields of social and community informatics, specialising in research relating to the effective use of information and communications technologies (ICTs) by communities and their members. Particular foci of his research include: ICTs as a form of mediated communication and the consequences of such use, for example by migrants and migrant groups; the use of ICTs by non-profit organisations and cultural institutions; and the role of social networks. He has also consulted widely in Australia and Vietnam, assisting libraries and non-profit organisations in making more effective use of ICT.

MANUELA FARINOSI PhD is post-doctoral researcher and adjunct professor of Economic Sociology at University of Udine (Italy). She received her PhD in Multimedia Communication in 2010. Her main research interests are focused on social and cultural aspects of digital technologies, with particular attention to the adoption and use of social media in the context of natural disasters. She has been Visiting Scholar at Ljubljana University (Slovenia), Alberta University (Canada), and Namur University (Belgium). She is currently a member of the COST Action FP1104.

Professor Leopoldina Fortunati is the director of the doctoral program in Multimedia Communication at the University of Udine (Italy), where she teaches Sociology of Communication and Culture. She has conducted research in the field of gender studies, cultural processes and communication and information technologies, and her works have been published in eleven languages. She is the Italian representative in the COST Domain Committee (ISCH, Individuals, Societies, Cultures and Health). She is associate editor of the journal The Information Society, and co-chair with Richard Ling of the Society for the Social Study of Mobile Communication (SSSMC).

Aldo de Moor is owner of the CommunitySense research consultancy company, founded in 2007. He earned his Ph.D. in Information Management from Tilburg University in the Netherlands in 1999. From 1999 to 2004, he worked as an assistant professor at the Department of Information Systems and Management at Tilburg University. From 2005 to 2006, he was a senior researcher at the Semantics Technology and Applications Research Laboratory (STARLab) of the Vrije Universiteit Brussel in Belgium. His research interests include community informatics, collaboration and communication modeling, socio-technical systems design, and the impact of ICT on society. See http://communitysense.nl/publ.html for his publications.

Tomi Oinas PhD is currently working as a postdoctoral researcher at the University of Jyväskylä, Finland. His research interests include job quality, working time, time use and division of labour in households.

Veli-Matti Salminen PhD works as a researcher at the Church Research Institute in Tampere, Finland. His PhD thesis was about the social differentiation of social networks in local communities. Salminen has studied different aspects of civil society. Currently, he is working on a research project that deals with the changing patterns of community in the Finnish Church.

Mauro Sarrica PhD in Personality and Social Psychology, researcher at the Department of Communication and Social Research, Sapienza, University of Rome (Italy). His main interests are social construction of knowledge, stability and change of social beliefs, and peace psychology. He has been involved in international and interdisciplinary research on Internet and Communication Technologies. In these fields he has studied the social representations of ICTs, the impact of the Internet on journalists' practices and the use of online forums to motivate and coordinate collective actions. His publications include twenty scientific papers on these topics and participation in international conferences.

Larry Stillman PhD is a Senior Research Fellow with the Centre for Organisational and Social Informatics (COSI) in the Faculty of IT at Monash University. He is interested in micro and macro level analysis and theorisation of the effect of technology in society, in both developed and developing countries. Research includes understandings of technology cultures in community based organisations in Australia; indigenous understandings of technology by Maori in New Zealand; and the social-technical effects of the Digital Doorway Initiative in South Africa and Australia. He is also researching information cultures in development NGOs and communities as part of the international Oxfam-Monash Partnership.

Sakari Taipale PhD works as an Academy of Finland Research Follow at the University of Jyväskylä (Finland). Taipale is also an Adjunct Professor at the University of Eastern Finland. His research interests relate to the uses and politics of new media technologies, on which topics he has published widely in international journals and edited volumes.

Emiliano Treré PhD is Associate Professor of Digital Media and Social Movements at the Faculty of Political and Social Sciences of the Autonomous University of Querétaro (Mexico). His work has been published in *New Media & Society*, the *International Journal of Communication*, *The Journal of Community Informatics*, the *ESSACHESS Journal for Communication Studies*, and in edited books in English, Spanish and Italian. He is currently concluding a two-year project where he explores Mexican movements' communication practices, with particular attention to social media platforms.

Jane Vincent PhD studies the social behaviours of ICT users, especially emotions and mobile communications. Jane is Senior Research Fellow in the Department of Media and Communication at the LSE and Visiting Fellow with the Digital World Research Centre, University of Surrey (UK). Her academic studies build on over 20 years within the mobile communications industry developing new products and services. Jane's publications include *Migration, Diaspora and Information Technology in Global Societies*, edited with L. Fortunati and R. Pertierra, and she is series editor of *Participation in Broadband Society*.

INTRODUCTION

Tom Denison, Mauro Sarrica and Larry Stillman

Community Informatics (CI) is the theory and practice of empowering communities with information and communication technologies and this overlaps with many of the research concerns of Social Informatics. There is a widespread expectation that CI will cultivate civic intelligence, enhance democracy, develop social capital, build communities, spur economies, empower individuals and groups, and result in many different forms of positive social change.

CI, in bringing together communities and technologies, works across at least three dimensions, though there may be others which are relevant:

- The Context and Values held by different stakeholders in CI
- The Processes and Methodologies which are brought to bear in CI enterprises
- The Systems (both technical and social) which influence CI and those which CI influences

Gurstein argues that the perspective of CI is unique, because the focus is upon *community* informatics rather than generic informatics as applied to communities or such fields as Social Informatics (Gurstein 2012, p. 44). However, the construct of "community" can be difficult to define and is sociologically well-problematised (Harvey 2000). Thus, the concept of "community" used within the framework of CI is fluid and highly contextualised, referring not just to local, geographic collectivities, but also more broadly to hybrid groups which form around shared beliefs, values, experiences, and interests and which have come to have a shared sense of identity or purpose in problem-solving. Such groups may have social, cultural, political, religious, class, gender, or racial dimensions, and are often in a situation of social, cultural, economic, or other disadvantage. They are usually not only the subjects of community-based CI initiatives but also partners. Communities may have long or short lives depending on their needs (Stillman & Stoecker 2008).

The focus on community ensures a strong practical focus and a concentration on developing strategies for using ICTs in building capacity and empowerment, for instance through telecentres, Community Multimedia Centres, and the like. A key concept in this regard is that of "effective use" developed by Gurstein in a critique of a research pre-occupation with the Digital Divide as ICT "access". Effective use is defined as "the capacity and opportunity to successfully integrate ICT into the accomplishment of self or collaboratively identified goals" (Gurstein 2007, p. 43).

"Effective use" emphasises the actual realisation of the potential benefits of ICTs and includes elements of practice, research and policy formulation. By and large, however, it is concerned with a combination of setting up the technical conditions for access to ICTs, and what Gurstien calls "social facilitation" or the provision of community and government support (Gurstein 2007, p. 43). A broad range of theory drawn from a variety of disciplines, such as sociology, planning, women's studies and library and information science contributes to the development of CI and underpin the development of a more reflective practice which looks past short term goals by taking into account broader societal concerns and contexts.

Multidisciplinary by nature, there has been some discussion as to whether a more rigorous definition or adaptation of a distinctive theory can bring CI's disparate elements together (see, for example, Stillman & Linger 2009), and provide a platform which will then be able to contribute to a more critically-oriented approach capable of better interacting with other disciplines. However, this view is contested by those who prefer to see it as a form of bricolage, where researchers and practitioners work together, drawing on specific theories and assembling methodologies from a wide array of available tools and approaches on a case-by-case basis. This volume is not intended to resolve that debate, but to reflect a range of approaches and research that contribute to the field – primarily from a European perspective. In particular, these studies do not represent the practitioner end of CI, but rather the theories which contribute to our understandings of ICTs and the meanings that people bring to socio-technical systems constructed using ICTs.

This book is thus intended to add some theoretical perspectives to the growing body of CI literature and as a supplement to some of the main sources (for example, *The Journal of Community Informatics*, or the annual *Proceedings of the Community Informatics Research Network (CIRN) Prato Conference*). Plans for the volume were first discussed late in 2011 at a workshop in Prato Italy, with participants drawn from two overlapping research communities: the first associated with COST research "Actions", particularly on the theme of the Broadband Society, and the second associated with the CIRN Prato conferences. The chapters as presented here have all undergone further development in the intervening time up to the publication of this volume.

Most of the chapters demonstrate a strong sociological influence, focusing in particular on the use of ICTs as tools for communications in a variety of contexts and from a variety of perspectives. Most also deal with methodological concerns and stress the fact that the online world and mobile communications devices cannot be isolated from overall communications practices.

In their chapter "Internet use and informal help for surrounding communities in Finland", Sakari Taipale, Tomi Oinas and Veli-Matti Salminen examine the question of sociability from a sociological perspective, and whether or not the adoption and use of ICTs weakens or strengthens the likelihood of a person providing help to others. Their primary interest in this is whether the use of ICTs, and social networking sites in particular, enhances or undermines social cohesion. The subject has previously drawn much attention (see, for example Zhao 2006) and could be seen as a core concern of those promoting the use of ICTs in a social setting. Their results support the argument that the Internet and social networking sites are not so much sources or generators for help, but tools that facilitate interaction.

Mauro Sarrica, Leopoldina Fortunati and Alberta Contarello continue the theme in their contribution "New technologies, ageing and social wellbeing in a southern Italian context". They are also concerned with questions of social inclusion and the elderly, but their focus is on two assumptions which often shape thinking in programs involving the elderly and new technologies: that new technologies can enhance social inclusion for the elderly; and that the elderly lack both the interest and the capacity to adopt new technologies. In order to address these assumptions, they examine how elderly people socially construct the meaning of the Internet and mobile phones and how the social representations of ICTs related to perceived social wellbeing. Their findings show that although they find support for the purported lack of interest and capacity in ICTs with regard to the Internet, that is not the case with regard to mobile phones. That is, the elderly are quite capable of distinguishing between new technologies and their utility with regard to their needs and goals and as a consequence the common assumption that the role of new technologies is "positive by definition" should be critically revisited.

The next two papers, by Francesca Comunello and by Manuela Farinosi and Emiliano Treré examine not just the use of Social Networking applications in disaster or crisis management, but also related methodological issues. Francesca Comunello, in her chapter "Studying crisis communications on social media", is particularly interested in developing a conceptual framework with which to analyse the role of social media in major crises. Her primary foci are on citizens' activities and on information spread and the dynamics of information diffusion from the perspective of emergency services and institutions. Starting from the methodological approaches and concerns developed in the field of Internet Studies, she emphasises that the whole media environment forms an ecosystem that cannot be understood in terms of individual applications, because each application offers different affordances which are best suited to a specific communications needs. Like all the authors in this volume, she also argues for stronger integration between practical and theoretical work, and between the online and offline worlds, adding a word of caution not to focus solely on the analysis of readily available large datasets of social media postings which, although offering unprecedented access, are difficult to analyse when divorced from their original context.

The need to study the whole communications ecosystem – both online and offline – is further developed in the subsequent chapter by Manuela Farinosi and Emiliano Treré: "Social movements, social media and post-disaster resilience". Using the events following the tragic 2009 earthquake in L'Aquila, a small city in the centre of Italy, they examine the interplay between a rapid increase in the use of the Internet technologies and social media by local citizens, and local activism. They argue that, unlike the dominant role that is frequently attributed to social media, what they call an "Integrated System of Local Protest" (ISoLP), based on crossovers between traditional media and multiple digital technologies, provides a more accurate portrayal of the complex communication ecology that arose. They further argue that while digital media creates new possibilities for mobilisation and organisation, "events, assemblies and informal meetings are still identified by the activists as crucial arenas where the bottom-up participation and the empowerment of citizens find their more complete realisation" (see this volume p. 81).

The final three chapters are more exploratory in nature. Aldo de Moor continues the theme of social networking / Web 2.0 applications in his chapter: "Expanding the academic research community". However, he turns the discussion away from academia and in a new direction by examining the growth of crowd sourcing and citizen science. He asks whether or not such practices might be harnessed in improving the quality and relevance of academic research. Placing academic research in the context of a range of current problems, he discusses the potential for a more collaborative and democratic form of research based on the use of social media tools and the development of new forms of collaboration between academia and other stakeholders in society. A variation of this approach is often required by the very nature of working within CI, and he argues that academia can generally benefit from this approach, the result being that research becomes more accountable, more sustainable, and more relevant to society's needs.

The final two papers, "What's so special about the mobile phone" by Jane Vincent and "Understanding the use of mobile phones in difficult circumstances" by Larry Stillman examine the phenomenon of the mobile phone, paying particular attention to the interplay between the meanings invested in them, emotional attachments to them, and their use. Using the UK as an example, Jane Vincent outlines developments in everyday communications over time before drawing on concepts of domestication (Silverstone & Hirsch 1992) and electronic emotion (Vincent & Fortunati 2009) to examine how issues such as emotional attachment have not only contributed to the ubiquitous presence of mobile phones in everyday life but have influenced the design of new products and services – a finding that should resonate with those designing socio-technical systems within the CI space.

Larry Stillman follows up on some of the themes raised in Jane Vincent's chapter, but in the context of a South African township where overwhelming disadvantage is compounded by isolation. He agrees that people form emotional attachments to mobile phones, but questions whether or not the mobile phone is the panacea it is often interpreted as in these settings, and whether or not it brings with it the same benefits as it does in more developed societies or countries. Using insights from critical and geographic theory, he argues that the utility of the mobile phone is contextualised by pervasive disruption in the lives of low-income people. He suggests that the mobile phone cannot bring the same benefits as they do to people in more advanced economies. Despite that, it still has a role to play, and his chapter serves to re-emphasise one of the main tenets of CI – that technological determinism and evangelism "devoid of social critique and social context" has no place in the theory and practice of CI.

References

Gurstein, M. (2007). *What is Community Informatics (and Why Does It Matter)?* Milan, Italy: Polimetrica.

Gurstein, M. (2012). Toward a conceptual framework for community informatics. In A. Clement, M. Gurstein, G. Longford, M. Moll & L. R. Shade (Eds.), *Connecting Canadians: Investigations in Community Informatics* (pp. 35–61). Edmonton: Athabasca University Press.

Harvey, D. (2000). *Possible Urban Worlds. The Fourth Megacities Lecture.* Amersfoort, The Netherlands: Twynstra Gudde Management Consultants.

Murdock, G., Hartmann, P., & Gray, P. (1992). Contextualizing home computing, resources and practices. In R. Silverstone & E. Hirsch (Eds.), *Consuming Technologies: Media and Information in Domestic Spaces* (pp. 146–160). London: Routledge.

Stillman, L., & Linger, H. (2009). Community informatics and information systems: How can they be better connected? *The Information Society, 25*(4), 1–10.

Stillman, L., & Stoecker, R. (2008). Community informatics. In G. D. Garson & M. Khosrow-Pour (Eds.), *Handbook of Research on Public Information Technology* (pp. 50–60). Hershey, PA: Idea Group.

Vincent, J., & Fortunati, L. (Eds.) (2009). *Electronic Emotion. The Mediation of Emotion via Information and Communication Technologies.* Oxford: Peter Lang.

Zhao, S. (2006). Do Internet users have more social ties? A call for differentiated analyses of Internet use. *Journal of Computer-Mediated Communication, 11*(3), 844–862.

Chapter 1

INTERNET USE AND INFORMAL HELP FOR SURROUNDING COMMUNITIES IN FINLAND

SAKARI TAIPALE, TOMI OINAS AND VELI-MATTI SALMINEN

This chapter investigates whether Internet use and involvement in social networking sites are related to the unpaid help that is provided to members of the surrounding communities. Three different forms of unpaid help are studied: assistance in care, housework and technology use. Previous literature dealing with the impacts of ICT use on the social cohesion of communities and the sense of togetherness is discussed to provide a solid basis for the research. As for the empirical part of the study, the chapter analyses the Finnish Time Use Survey collected between 2009 and 2010. The results show that it is not Internet use per se that is associated with the provision of informal help to the other members of a neighbouring community. Rather, it is the social use of the Internet which is positively associated with the informal help given to others in the offline context. However, Internet use may also add to informal help, provided face-to-face, but only when the help is given in technology use. The study suggest that the social benefits of Internet use, and especially those of online social networking, for communities are strongly segmented according to the type of help provision.

Introduction

For many years, sociological studies have investigated whether the adoption and use of information and communication technologies (ICTs) have weakened or reinforced people's sociability. The development of the Internet from the platform that people use to store information and cognise what others publish (Web 1.0) to a collaborative (Web 2.0) and co-operative tool (Web 3.0, Fuchs 2008, 2010, Web squared, O'Reilly & Battelle 2009) emphasised the need to study the relationship between Internet use and sociability from new perspectives. Previous results dealing with Internet use in general have remained somewhat contradictory (e.g. DiMaggio et al. 2001, Wellman et al. 2001, Nie & Lutz 2002, Nie et al. 2002, Fortunati et al. 2012) and the reflections on whether the changes in sociability levels benefit the community in which the use of ICT takes place has not received much scientific attention. More recently, scholars have also noted that it is perhaps not the use of ICTs as such, but rather the ways and purposes of usage that matter. The social and collaborative functions of the Internet form the basis of these studies. For instance, Zhao (2006) has made a distinction between solitary online activities, such as Web surfing and news reading that do not involve direct contact with other people, and social activities, such as e-mailing and chatting, where other people engage in online interaction. In his study, the social users of the Internet had more social ties than non-users. It is against this backcloth that we are curious to investigate whether people who use the social functions of the Internet are also more likely to assist their close friends and neighbours on a voluntary basis.

In this study we will investigate whether Internet use and involvement in social networking sites are related to the unpaid help that is provided to members of the surrounding communities. This is to determine whether the use of the Internet in general or the social use of the Internet in particular, or perhaps both, is associated with the help provided to others. Furthermore, we will explore whether Internet use and engagement in social networking sites are similarly connected to three different forms of informal help: assistance in care, housework and technology use. From the perspective of community and social informatics, these questions are perennially interesting since ICT can both enhance and undermine the social cohesion of communities and affect the sense of togetherness (e.g. Putnam 2000, Turkle 2011). Considering ageing populations in Europe, there is considerable pressure to promote the use of informal care and unpaid help in order to keep the public expenditures on social services and health care under control.

The empirical results of this study are drawn from the Finnish Time Use Survey collected between 2009 and 2010. With the help of this extensive data set, consisting of both time use diaries and personal interview questionnaires, we are able to elaborate the relationship between Internet use and unpaid help provision in Finland. The data includes both household and individual level information. In terms of methodology, both descriptive and multivariate statistics are summarised. Finland is a country with one of the most rapidly ageing populations in Europe. It also has one of the highest participation rates in voluntary activities in Europe (McCloughan et al. 2011). When it is considered that Finland's information society infrastructures are relatively advanced and citizens have good access to the Internet (78% of the entire population, Statistics Finland 2011), we believe that Finland serves as a good case for investigating the relationship between Internet usage and unpaid help.

The rest of this chapter is organised as follows. First, there is an overview of recent literature on help provision, and the main socio-demographic predictors of help are summarised. After that, the previous research on the relationship between ICT use and social interaction in general is summarised. Then the chapter proceeds to discuss the concept of community and how it has received further definitions with the rise of new ICTs. The literature review finishes with the formulation of hypotheses for this study. The data, measures and statistic tools exploited are then presented before discussing the results. The chapter concludes by summarising the empirical results and considers whether the use of the Internet and social networking sites is beneficial to informal help provision within communities.

Previous literature

The different forms of help

Prior literature makes distinctions regarding the provision of help. First, formal help provided through institutionalised actors, both public and private, is typically separated from informal help – alternatively conceptualised as unpaid labour – provided by family members, friends and neighbours (e.g. van Groenou et al. 2006, p. 747, Kahn et al. 2011, p. 78). However, the conceptual boundary between the two has been questioned by arguing that formal caregivers may also become personally attached to the recipients of care (Kröger 2009, pp. 400–401). Second, empirical studies make a distinction between the recipients of assistance: care help can be targeted at both relatives and non-relatives (Kahn et al. 2011, p. 78). Some prior accounts have noted that different forms of help tend to be shared with either kin or non-kin contacts, but rarely with both (Gallagher & Gerstel 2001, Salminen 2012). In practice, informal assistance may work as an alternative to formal care or can, as often is the case, be provided and received to supplement inadequacies in formal help. In this study, we focus on informal help provided to neighbours, friends and co-workers (i.e. non-relatives), who are viewed as comprising the surrounding community of a help provider.

At the operational level, informal help is typically divided into parts according to the type of help activity. In this study we divide informal help into three subcategories: housework, care work and help in technology use. *Housework* comprises cooking, housekeeping, maintenance, shopping and errands and related travels (Shelton & John 1996, Robinson & Godbey 1999, Gershuny 2000). We examine *care work* separately from housework as research literature shows that care work is considered more rewarding than housework and maintenance tasks, and this is reflected in the differences in the perceived pleasantness of these tasks (Sullivan 1996, Robinson & Godbey 1999). Despite these differences, housework and caregiving are also linked to each other. For instance, cooking and washing up often take place simultaneously with the child care. It is also interesting to note that help in housework and care have been found to be the most common types of help within social support networks. Furthermore, they are exchanged more typically between close relatives than acquaintances such as community members (van der Gaag 2005, p. 159). As the third subcategory, we analyse *help in technology use* separately from other forms of informal help. This is because literature reveals the importance of social support networks for the take up and use of new communication technology. Arguably, people are more likely to give up a new technology if they have no friends or neighbours from whom to request support in use (Murdock et al. 1992, Hargittai 2003).

Previous literature is also illustrative of the predictors of informal help. As regards *gender*, men provide less assistance than women, which partly derives from men's higher labour market participation rates and more secure employment positions (Bracke et al. 2008) as well as from culturally-produced views of what tasks are proper for men and women (Shelton & John 1996). The impact of *age* seems to differ. Some studies indicate that older people help fewer non-relatives than younger ones (Gallagher 1994), whereas others have found that older adults (50–64 year-olds) are the most helpful group in this respect (Bracke et al. 2008). *Education* has proved to be a rather consistent predictor and a stronger one than income. Higher levels of education are linked to more help supplied to non-relatives (Gallagher 1994, Bracke et al. 2008). *Marital status* is also found to condition the provision of help to non-kin. Married people provide less support to non-kin than unmarried people, which is probably related to their time-consuming responsibilities at home (e.g. child-rearing) (Kahn et al. 2011). In addition to marital status, the presence of dependent children also decreases the provision of care to non-relatives, although the effects have been considerably small and gendered (dependent children affect more the help given by women than that of men) (Bracke et al. 2008, Kahn et al. 2011). Moreover, *employment* status has been found to be weakly associated with the informal help to non-relatives. Employed people provide help to others slightly more than those who are currently not employed (e.g. unemployed, students and housewives or husbands) (Kahn et al. 2011).

The relationship between ICT use and social interaction

At the turn of the 21st century, sociologists began to contemplate the possible impacts of technology use on physically co-present social intercourse. Robert D. Putnam's (2000) analysis of the decline of the American community was one of the main promoters of this debate. He considered that "individualising" technologies, such as television and probably also the Internet, whose possible impact on social interaction was difficult to foresee at that time, would diminish people's civic engagement and activity. A few years earlier, Graham and Marvin (1996, p. 207) had already anticipated a shift towards home-centredness which, according to them, resulted from advances in telecommunications and more individualised services targeted at households. In fact, some early accounts on the use of the Internet seemed to provide support for these arguments. Internet use was considered to have a "displacement effect" on physically proximate interactions and, hence, time online was even seen as an asocial activity (e.g. Nie & Lutz 2002, Nie et al. 2002).

Later, many studies showed that Internet users actually have larger social networks than non-users (e.g. DiMaggio et al. 2001, Wellman et al. 2001). In some more sophisticated analyses, possible modifying factors have been controlled. For instance, Zhao (2006, p. 13) showed that the type of online activities and the amount of time people spend on these activities are connected to offline social connection. People who use the Internet for interpersonal contact (e.g. email and chat) are more likely to engage in larger social circles offline than those who use it for solitary purposes (e.g. Web surfing). Also Petrič's (2006) study stresses the importance of the differences between social uses of the Internet and instrumental uses, where the Internet appears as a mean of achieving personal goals. Fortunati et al. (2013) show that in the five largest European Union countries the overall volume of people's sociability actually remained quite stable between 1996 and 2009. While mobile phones and PCs were associated with the increase in sociability in 1996, the Internet was an ICT that particularly added to people's sociability in 2009. Taken all together, these results demonstrate that there is no single, but many, Internet effects (Wellman et al. 2001, p. 451). It might well be that, in particular, the social uses of the Internet add to social intercourse, and hence are also positively associated with the provision of informal help. This puzzling controversy between previous findings partly results from different research designs and indicators employed in the studies (cf. Zhao 2006).[1]

Community reconsidered

New ICTs that make possible social interaction and the sense of community at distance have forced social scientists to think over the sufficiency of the classical definitions of "community". The concept of community has been largely defined by stressing either social relations within a certain geographical area or belonging to a group which is included in the community (Stacey 1969, 135). In their definition of community as a totality, Cnaan et al. (2008) named three elements: shared ecology (with place and location defining and restricting social life), social organisation and shared cultural and symbolic meanings. Of these three elements of community, the second, social organisation, consists of mobilisation, the formation of new social networks, and the possession of social capital.

Thus, community does have an element comprising social ties as such with no geographical or territorial limitations. In other words, social ties and networks are more or less essential for a local community to develop, but social networks can be autonomous from a certain area or location. A good example of this has resulted from the rise of Internet technology. The concept of community is stretched to cover the idea of virtual communities where people can gather together online regardless of their physical locations. Bearing this in mind, Hampton (2003) has proposed new dimensions to the concept of community. He puts forward the idea that "community" could be seen as consisting of concatenating social ties that make up networks of sociability, help and support.

Taking Hampton's proposal into consideration, this study builds on a data-driven conceptualisation of community. The community is viewed

---

[1]   For instance, Nie et al. (2002) studied diary-based time use with a sample targeted at approximately 6,000 Americans between the ages of 18 and 64. In comparison, many findings presented by Wellman and his colleagues are based on a single specific residential community called "Netville". The number of respondents included in their analyses has often been considerably small; 109 homes with 52 participants who were "connected" and 21 who were "not connected" (Wellman et al. 2001, Hampton & Wellman 2003, Hampton 2007). In addition, Nie et al. utilised time-use indicators (e.g. time online and activity time with family, friends and so on), but Wellman et al. accounted for the number of people who were at least recognised, talked with and visited.

as consisting of neighbours, friends and co-workers to whom assistance in housework, care and technology use is provided. As defined in relation to these three groups of people, community emerges as a relatively broad concept. It does not include the idea of strong shared values, which would produce social cohesion, but it is not based on pure self-interest either as the provision of help must be gratuitous by nature. However, our application of community relates to the idea of network-based social capital, which considers network contacts as channels mediating different kinds of resources and thus takes into account the potential assets embedded in the network contacts (Lin 2007). As regards the character of social contacts, we concentrate in this study on informal contacts. Contrary to voluntary work channelled through formal organisations, informal help given to a near community is personal in character and does not necessarily involve any mediating organisations.

Research hypotheses

By focusing on the help provided to members of a surrounding community, this study makes inroads into a less studied field of social and community informatics. Due to a lack of previous research results dealing with the relationship between Internet use and informal help (other than civic participation), hypotheses are based on the above-reviewed literature. As the most recent and convincing research results argue that Internet use – the social uses of the Internet in particular – enhances social interaction in physically proximate relations, we expect that:

> H1) The frequency of Internet use increases the provision of informal help for surrounding communities.

> H2) Engagement in social networking sites increases the provision of informal help more than the overall frequency of Internet use.

To elaborate further, the connection between Internet use and the provision of help for neighbouring communities, we divide the measure of overall help into three parts: help in care, housework and technology use. As the frequency of Internet use and engagement in social networking sites are likely to be more strongly connected to the assistance in technological use than to the help in care and homework, we expect to see that:

> H3) Internet use and involvement in social networking sites increase all three forms of help, yet the connection is stronger as regards help in technology use.

Data and methods

Data

The analysis is based on the latest Finnish Time Use Survey (FTUS) collected in 2009–2010 by Statistics Finland. The FTUS is an extensive interview survey in which all members (over 10 years old) of participating households keep accurate diaries on their time use during one weekday and one weekend day. The FTUS was collected by using a two-phase, single stage cluster sample, in which households served as clusters and individuals were elementary units. The data includes 7,480 recorded diary days and 3,795 interviewed respondents from 2,614 different households. The FTUS is part of the Harmonised European Time Use Survey (HETUS), coordinated by Eurostat and the University of Essex. The interview data includes information about the main activity (employed, unemployed, studying, etc.), working hours (length, pattern), voluntary work, hobbies and health (altogether 111 questions). In the interview data, each person is also asked to report for what purposes and how often they use a computer or the Internet and if they are using social media, that is if they are members of social networks such as Facebook or MySpace. In this study, the sub-sample of over 15-year-old respondents is analysed by utilising the information from the interview questions (n=3444).[2] Younger respondents are excluded from the analysis as they are clearly nett recipients of unpaid help. Table 1.1 presents descriptive statistics on the sample.

Table 1.1. Sociodemographic characteristics of respondents

Variable		Mean (std. dev.) or %	Unweighted N
Age		48.3 (18.8)	3,444
Gender	Male	47.6%	1,608
	Female	52.4%	1,836
Education	Primary	30.6%	915
	Secondary	40.4%	1,318
	Tertiary	28.9%	1,211

---

2   We use specific methods designed for analysing complex samples (PASW 18.0 Complex Samples package) in order to account for the sampling design in FTUS. If estimation is done by assuming a simple random sample, the obtained estimates are likely to be biased (Landis et al. 1982, Lehtonen & Pahkinen 2004).

Variable		Mean (std. dev.) or %	Unweighted N
Employment status	Employee	55.0%	1,993
	Unemployed	6.4%	157
	Student	7.7%	264
	Retired	28.3%	943
	Housewife	2.2%	74
	Other	0.3%	13
Dependent children	No	76.6%	2,461
	Yes	23.4%	983
Marital status	Not married	37.2%	869
	Married or cohabiting	62.8%	2,563

Measures

In the interview data each respondent was asked to report how frequently he or she uses the Internet. The response scale for Internet use ranged from 1="Never" to 6="Daily". In addition, respondents were asked about their social media usage: "Are you are a registered user of social networking sites (e.g. Facebook or MySpace)?" (see Table 1.2). This question was asked only of those who reported having used the Internet at least once or twice a year. The social networking measure was recoded afterwards so that those who reported not having used the Internet received the value zero.

In the interviews, respondents were also asked whether they had provided unpaid help to other households during the last four weeks in the following activities: childcare, caring for sick or elderly, cooking, cleaning, gardening, shopping and services, repairs and construction, car and bicycle maintenance, caring for pets, transportation and removals, and technology use. For each category of unpaid help, respondents were also asked to report to whom they provided help: relatives (broken down into the following categories: parents, adult children, children, siblings, grand children, other relatives); neighbours, friends or colleagues; and other people. From these questions, dichotomy indices for three different forms of informal help given to members of the surrounding community (i.e. neighbours, friends or colleagues) were constructed: assistance in care (including childcare and caring for sick or elderly), housework (including cooking, cleaning, gardening, shopping and services, repairs and construction, car and bicycle maintenance, caring for pets, transportation and removals) and technology use (including computer use and digital television). In addition, an aggregate measure of whether any informal help was provided to the surrounding community was created by combining the three indices.

Respondents' gender, age, educational level, marital status, presence of dependent children and employment status were used as controls in the statistical models. In previous studies, these factors were identified as important predictors of the provided informal help, as was presented above.

Statistical procedures

This study employs both descriptive and multivariate statistics. Three logistic regression models are conducted separately for each measure of informal help: the first model includes only Internet use, in the second model engagement in social networking sites and in the third model controls for background factors (gender, age, education, marital status, presence of dependent children and employment status) were added as covariates. This strategy allows comparison between the effects of Internet use and involvement in social networking sites before and after accounting for other factors.

Results

Descriptive results

Table 1.2 presents descriptive statistics on Internet use, social networking site memberships and the provision of informal help. The measure of frequency of Internet use shows a rather bipolar distribution: almost one-fourth never uses the Internet and almost half use it daily. However, using the Internet only occasionally is very rare. It seems that people either use the Internet quite frequently or not at all. Less than a third of respondents are registered as a member in social networking sites. This proportion is rather high as the sample is representative of the whole population. However, being a registered user does not yet indicate how actively these sites are used in practice. Based on previous studies (Smith & Rainie 2010) we can assume that there are also many respondents who have registered with these sites, but have never started to use them. Table 1.2 also shows that one-fourth of respondents have provided unpaid help to the members of the surrounding community. Most of this help seems to be in the form of housework activities. By contrast, helping the members of the surrounding communities in care duties and technology use are quite rare activities.

All covariates were significantly associated with both frequency of Internet and social networking site use, especially age and employment situation (not presented in the tables). For instance, as regards to age, the above mentioned bipolar distribution of Internet use is chiefly a product of age distribution. The share of Internet non-users increases and that of daily users decreases steadily with age; while about 80 per cent of 16 to 24 year-olds use the Internet daily, over 80 per cent of those aged 64 years or more did not use the Internet at all. In addition, of all covariates, age was most strongly associated with both social networking and informal help. As to employment situation, retired people differ from all other groups as 60 per cent of them never use the Internet. Similarly, over 96 per cent of retirees are not members of social networking sites.

Table 1.2. Descriptive statistics on Internet use, social networking and informal help

Variable		Percentage	Unweighted N
How often uses Internet	Never	22.9%	669
	Once or twice a year	1.6%	46
	At least once a month	3.0%	104
	Once or twice a week	11.2%	404
	Several days a week	13.4%	487
	Daily	48.0%	1,550
Member of social networking sites*	No	69.7%	2,347
	Yes	30.3%	913
Has helped neighbours, friends or colleagues in general	No	74.4%	2,610
	Yes	25.6%	834
Has helped neighbours, friends or colleagues in housework	No	78.8%	2,734
	Yes	21.2%	710
Has helped neighbours, friends or colleagues in care	No	93.6%	3,240
	Yes	6.4%	204
Has helped neighbours, friends or colleagues in technology use	No	96.3%	3,342
	Yes	3.7%	102

* Asked only of those who report using the Internet at least once or twice a year

Internet use and social networking site involvement as the predictors of informal help

The results of the logistic regression models predicting the provision of informal help in general are presented in Table 1.3. It shows that Internet use has a strong positive effect on informal help, but this effect is reduced when introducing the measure of social networking sites to the model. More interestingly, the effect of Internet use completely disappears when background factors are controlled in the model. However, the positive coefficient of social networking on informal help remains significant, although its level of significance decreases. Age, gender and marital status also have significant effects on overall informal help. Older people, females and married persons were less likely to provide unpaid help to members of their community. After examining the model in more detail, it was found that age was the single most important factor reducing the effects of both Internet use and social networking. As was noted earlier, the age of respondent was strongly connected to Internet use, social networking and informal help. This result clearly indicates the importance of controlling for age differences when studying effects of Internet or other ICT use on informal help. Older people are less likely to provide informal help to others, use the Internet and to be registered members of social networking sites. These results clearly oppose H1, which has to be rejected. However, these results provide support for H2; it is not Internet use per se but the social uses of the Internet that increase the provision of informal, unpaid help to other people.

Table 1.3. The effects of Internet use and involvement in social networking sites on informal help

Predictors	Model 1	Model 2	Model 3
Internet use	0.17***	0.10**	0.04
Social networking		0.58***	0.38**
Age			-0.01*
Male (ref.= female)			0.26**
Tertiary education (ref.= primary)			0.17
Secondary education (ref.= primary)			0.21
Employee (ref.= all others)			0.07
Married (ref.= not married)			-0.38**
Children (ref.= no children)			0.16
Constant	-1.59***	-1.56***	-0.89**
Nagelkerke's pseudo R^2	0.029	0.046	0.067
N	3,260	3,260	3,260

Estimates are regression coefficients from logistic regression analysis
Statistical significance: * $p < 0.05$, ** $p < 0.01$, *** $p < 0.001$

Next, the study examines informal help in more detail by conducting the same analysis separately for the three sub-categories of informal help: help in care, housework and technology use. The third hypothesis stated that Internet use and social networking is supposed to have a stronger connection with help provided in technology use. The results presented in Table 1.4 are partly supportive of this claim. In fact, after controlling for background factors, the frequency of Internet use is connected *only* to informal help given in technology use. Also, the social use of the Internet (i.e. involvement in social networking sites) has a clearly stronger effect on help given in technology use than on any other forms of informal help. Gender and marital status also play a major role in predicting help provided in technology use, education to a lesser extent. Not surprisingly, men and singles are clearly more likely to give help in this domain. Those with higher education are also more inclined to provide help in technology use than respondents with primary education only.

In addition to technology use, membership in social networking sites also increases slightly the probability of providing informal help in housework. However, age and gender seem to be more important factors for help in housework. Again, older people and females are less likely to provide help in this domain. Also, married people probably give less help in housework duties. The direction of gender differences in housework help may seem at first glance rather surprising. However, it should be noted that many of the duties belonging to this category are in fact repairs and other maintenance work, which men are more often responsible for than women (Robinson & Godbey 1999, Sayer 2010).

Neither Internet use in general nor the social use of it increases the probability of giving help in caring for children or older people. The significant positive effects of both Internet use and social networking are again reduced mainly due to the introduction of age, and to a lesser extent gender, to the model. Age, gender, and presence of dependent children are the most important factors explaining help in care work. As was the case with technology and housework, older people are less likely, and women and those who have their own children more likely to help others in care work.

In response to H3, the results presented here confirm that involvement in social networking sites increases the provision of unpaid help more than the frequency of Internet use. However, the effect of social networking site involvement was statistically significant only in the case of providing help in technology use and housework. Respectively, the effect of Internet use was significant only in the case of help given in technology use. Furthermore, it is worth noting that the predictive capacity (Nagelkerke's pseudo R^2) of the full models ranged from 4.7 per cent to 26.4 per cent of total variance. The highest figure was received by the model where the provision of help in technology use was explained.

Table 1.4. The effects of Internet use and social networking on informal help in care, housework and technology use

Predictors	Help in care			Help in housework			Help in technology use		
	Model 1	Model 2	Model 3	Model 1	Model 2	Model 3	Model 1	Model 2	Model 3
Internet use	0.21***	0.15*	0.11	0.11***	0.06	-0.01	0.85***	0.65**	0.55**
Social networking		0.46*	0.18		0.49***	0.27*		1.15**	1.10**
Age			-0.01***			-0.01**			-0.01
Male (ref.= female)			-0.85***			0.28**			1.75***
Tertiary education (ref.= primary)			-0.15			0.21			1.11*
Secondary education (ref.= primary)			-0.40			0.25			0.97*
Employee (ref.= all others)			-0.20			0.12			-0.52
Married (ref.= not married)			-0.04			-0.33*			-1.15***
Children (ref.= no children)			0.89***			0.03			-0.18
Constant	-3.40***	-3.36***	-2.12***	-1.65***	1.62***	-0.93**	-6.87***	-6.60***	-6.78***
Nagelkerke's pseudo R^2	0.022	0.029	0.089	0.013	0.024	0.047	0.107	0.143	0.264
N	3,260	3,260	3,260	3,260	3,260	3,260	3,260	3,260	3,260

Estimates are regression coefficients from logistic regression analysis
Statistical significance: * $p < 0.05$, ** $p < 0.01$, *** $p < 0.001$

Concluding remarks

This chapter aimed to determine whether Internet use and involvement in social networking sites are related to the unpaid help that is provided to the members of surrounding communities. The rationale of this study relates to the fact that today, people in affluent Western countries have relatively easy access to the Internet and social media. Additionally, the time people spend by using these new ICTs can either end up "stealing" time from face-to-face interactions with neighbours and friends or people's online sociality may have positive spill-over effects on offline sociability, such as the provision of informal help. Furthermore, the study explored whether Internet use and engagement in social networking sites are similarly connected to help given in care, housework and technology use.

The results of the study show that it is not Internet use per se that is associated with the provision of informal help to the other members of a neighbouring community. Rather, it is the social use of the Internet which is positively associated with the informal help given to others in the offline context. This result, which supports the simple fact that social people are social both online and offline, corroborates what Zhao (2006) and others have argued earlier; social activities preformed online are connected to people's sociability in physically proximate relations. Instead, the results presented in this chapter question the relevance of the perennial debate on whether the Internet use increases or decreases people's sociability (e.g. DiMaggio et al. 2001, Wellman et al. 2001, Nie & Lutz 2002, Nie et al. 2002). In the light of this study, Internet use may add to informal help provided face-to-face, but only when the help is given in technology use.

This study refines previous research results by disaggregating the applied indicator of sociability, namely the provision of informal help, in three sub-categories. The results, controlled for socio-demographic variables, clearly indicated that it is solely help in technology use that is affected by Internet use. As regards help in care and housework, the connection disappeared when socio-demographic factors were controlled. In contrast, the membership of social networking sites does slightly increase the informal help provided in housework. If we had only looked at the overall provision of help, results would have been skewed by the fact that the increase in overall help is largely accounted for by help in technology use. This result is in line with common sense as well; those who can use the Internet and social networking sites are also competent at providing assistance with technological problems to others.

All in all, the results of this study suggest that the social benefits of Internet use, and especially those of online social networking for communities, are strongly segmented according to the type of help provision. The results also reveal that Internet use and involvement in social networking sites may indicate user sociability. They are tools for interaction rather than sources or generators of any substantial increase in help provided to the surrounding communities. In this study, the community was defined broadly by referring to neighbours, friends and co-workers who make up the networks of sociability, help and support. The results are also likely to depend on a country context, which makes us call for more analyses from cross-national perspectives. In the future, more detailed analysis of the social consequences of Internet use, which clearly takes into account to whom the help is provided, is required.

References

Arnkil, R. (2012). *EEO Review: Employment policies to improve active ageing.* Finland: European Employment Observatory.

Bracke, P., Christiaens, W., & Wauterickx, N. (2008). The pivotal role of women in informal care. *Journal of Family Issues, 29*(10), 348–1378.

Cnaan, R.A., Milofsky, C., & Hunter, A. (2008). Creating a frame for understanding local organizations. In R.A. Cnaan & C. Milofsky (Eds.), *Handbook of Community Movements and Local Organizations* (pp. 1–19). New York: Springer.

DiMaggio, P., Hargittai, E., Russell Neuman, W.R., & Robinson, J.P. (2001). Social implications of the Internet. *Annual Review of Sociology, 1*, 307–336.

Fortunati, L., Taipale, S., & de Luca, F. (2013). What happened to body-to-body sociability? *Social Science Research, 42*(3), 893–905.

Fuchs, C. (2010). Social software and Web 2.0. Their sociological foundation and implications. In S. Murugesan (Ed.), *Handbook of Research on Web 2.0, 3.0 and x.0: Technologies, Business and Social Application* (pp. 764–798). Hershey, PA: Information Science References.

Gallagher, S.K. (1994). Doing their share: Comparing patterns of help given by older and younger adults. *Journal of Marriage and Family, 56*(3), 567–578.

Gallagher, S.K., & Gerstel, N. (2001). Connections and constraints: The effects of children on caregiving. *Journal of Marriage and Family, 61*(3), 265–275.

Gershuny, J. (2000). *Changing Times. Work and Leisure in Postindustrial Society.* Oxford: Oxford University Press.

Graham, S., & Marvin, S. (1996). *Telecommunication and the City. Electronic Spaces, Urban Places.* London: Routledge.

Hampton, K. (2003). Grieving for a lost network: Collective action in a wired suburb. *The Information Society, 19*(5), 417–428.

Hampton, K., & Wellman, B. (2003). Neighboring in Netville: How the Internet supports community and social capital in a wired suburb. *City and Community, 2*(4), 277–311.

Hampton, K.N. (2007). Neighborhoods in the network society: The e-neighbors study. *Information, Communication & Society, 10*(5), 714–748.

Hargittai, E. (2003). The digital divide and what to do about it. In D. C. Jones (Ed.), *The New Economy Handbook* (pp. 100–120). San Diego: Academic Press.

Ishii-Kuntz, M., & Coltrane, S. (1992). Predicting the share of household labor: Are parenting and housework distinct? *Sociological Perspectives, 35*(4), 629–647.

Kahn, J.R., McGill, B.S., & Bianchi, S.M. (2011). Help to family and friends: Are there gender differences at older ages? *Journal of Marriage and Family, 73*(1), 77–92.

Kröger, T. (2009). Care research and disability studies: Nothing in common? *Critical Social Policy, 29*, 398–420.

Landis, R.J., Lepkowski, J.M., Eklund, S.A., & Stehouwer, S.A. (1982). A statistical methodology for analyzing data from a complex survey. The first national health and nutrition examination survey. *Data from the National Health Survey, 2*(92). Hyattsville, Maryland: National Center for Health Statistics.

Lehtonen, R., & Pahkinen, E. (2004). *Practical Methods for Design and Analysis of Complex Surveys* (2nd ed.). Chichester: Wiley.

Lin, N. (2007). Building a network theory of social capital. In N. Lin, K. Cook & R. S. Burt (Eds.), *Social Capital: Theory and Research* (pp. 3–29). New Brunswick: Transaction Publishers.

McCloughan, P.B., Batt, W.H., Costine, M; Scully, D. (2011). *Second European quality of life survey. Participation in volunteering and unpaid work*. Dublin, Ireland: European Foundation for the Improvement of Living and Working Conditions

Murdock, G., Hartmann, P., Gray, P. (1992). Contextualizing home computing, resources and practices. In R. Silverstone & E. Hirsch (Eds.), *Consuming Technologies: Media and Information in Domestic Spaces* (pp. 146–160). London: Routledge.

Nie, N.H., & Erbirng, L. (2002). Internet and society: A preliminary report. Stanford, CA: Stanford Institute for the Quantitative Study of Society.

Nie, N.H., Hillygus, D.S., & Erbring, L. (2002). Internet use, interpersonal relations, and sociability: A time diary study. In B. Wellman & C. Haythornthwaite (Eds.), *The Internet in Everyday Life* (Vol. I, pp. 215–243). Malden: Blackwell.

O'Reilly, T., & Battelle, J. (2009). *Web Squared: Web 2.0 Five Years On. Paper*. Paper presented at the Web 2.0 Summit Special Oct 20-22 2009, San Francisco, CA.

Petrič, G. (2006). Conceptualizing and measuring the social uses of the Internet: The case of personal web sites. *The Information Society, 22*(5), 291–301.

Putnam, R. (2000). *Bowling Alone: The Collapse and Revival of American Community*. NY: Simon and Schuster.

Robinson, J.P., & Godfrey, G. (1999). *Time for Life: The Surprising Ways Americans Use Their Time*. (2nd ed.). University Park: The Pennsylvania State University Press.

Salminen, V.-M. (2012). *Verkostot, paikallisuus ja eriarvoisuus [Networks, locality and inequality]*. (PhD), University of Jyväskylä, Jyväskylä.

Sayer, L.C. (2010). Trends in housework. In J. Treas & S. Drobnic (Eds.), *Dividing the Domestic: Men, Women & Household Work in Cross-National Perspective* (pp. 19–40). Stanford: Stanford University Press.

Shelton, B.A., & John, D. (1996). The division of household labor. *Annual Review of Sociology, 22*(1), 299–322.

Smith, A., & Lee, R. (2011). 8% of online Americans use Twitter. *Pew Research Center's Internet & American Life Project*. Washing DC: Pew Research Center.

Stacey, M. (1969). The myth of community studies. *British Journal of Sociology, 20*(2), 134–147.

Sullivan, O. (1996). Time co-ordination, the domestic division of labour and affective relations: Time use and the enjoyment of activities within couples. *Sociology, 30*(1), 79–100.

Taipale, S. (2013). Mobilities in Finland's information society strategies from 1995 to 2010. *Mobilities, 8*(2), 293–211.

Turkle, S. (2011). *Alone Together. Why We Expect More from Technology and Less from Each Other*. NY: Basic Books.

van der Gaag, M. (2005). *Measurement of Individual Social Capital*. Amsterdam: NWO.

van Groenou, M.B., Glaser, K., Tommassini, C., & Jacobs, T. (2006). Socio-economic status differences in older people's use of informal and formal help: A comparison of four European countries. *Ageing & Society, 26*(5), 745–766.

Wellman, B., Quan Haase, A., Witte, J., & Hampton, K. (2001). Does the Internet increase, decrease, or supplement social capital? Social networks, participation, and community commitment. *American Behavioral Scientist, 45*(3), 436–455.

Zhao, S. (2006). Do Internet users have more social ties? A call for differentiated analyses of Internet use. *Journal of Computer-Mediated Communication, 11*(3), 844–862.

Chapter 2

NEW TECHNOLOGIES, AGEING AND SOCIAL WELLBEING IN A SOUTHERN ITALIAN CONTEXT

Mauro Sarrica, Leopoldina Fortunati
and Alberta Contarello

The chapter questions two assumptions which concern elderly people and technologies. First, that the impact of new technologies is by definition positive for their wellbeing; and second, that the elderly suffer from a digital divide because they lack the interest in and cognitive capacities to adjust to these new technologies. In order to address these assumptions this chapter investigates how elderly people socially construct the meaning of the Internet and mobile phones and how their social representations are related with perceived social wellbeing. A questionnaire which includes free association tasks, measures wellbeing and collects information on use practices was distributed to 100 elderly people living in small- and medium-sized villages in the region of Puglia, South Italy. The results indicate that the relationship between new technologies and social wellbeing is not automatically positive and that elderly people play an active role in choosing and interpreting new technologies.

Introduction

The present paper aims to explore how elderly people socially construct the meaning of new technologies – namely the mobile phone and the Internet – and how this social construction is related to their perceived social wellbeing. This point is central to the understanding of the so-called digital divide between the elderly and broader society.

Policy interventions aimed at improving the quality of life among elderly people in many cases continue to be based on two assumptions. First, the role of new technologies is considered by definition positive and thus as a consequence it is expected that these technologies should be used as broadly as possible to achieve the greatest benefit possible. Second, the elderly suffer from a digital divide because they are less interested in new technologies (while being at the cutting edge of older technologies, such as TV) than other age groups and/or because they do not possess the cognitive capacities to use them. These assumptions have the effect of creating paradoxical expectations that the elderly should become equal to the young and devote themselves to gaining at least a basic level of understanding of new technologies, even though their lives and needs are specific and different.

These two assumptions continue to dominate the political debate, although they have been implicitly contested by at least three strands of research.

The first strand is provided by the application of psychological models to studies on the elderly understood as an age group (Baltes & Baltes 1990, Carstensen 1991, 1993, Gergen & Gergen 2002). This strand of studies has shown that ageing is not necessarily characterised by cognitive and physical decay. The elderly in fact develop coping strategies in compensation, as well as the capacity to set goals so as to optimise their wellbeing.

The second strand of studies includes research on the relationship between factors such as habits, rewards, attitudes and emotions, and the lack of use of new technologies, as well as previous investigations on social representations of information and communications technologies (Contarello et al. 2007, Contarello & Sarrica, 2007). From these studies it emerges that the elderly are not a passive target of new technologies.

The third strand is made up of sociological studies that have taken a critical stance toward technological determinism, such as those carried out by Stevenson (2009) or that by Sourbati (2008), according to whom "policy development must abandon its technology-centric focus and take a broader, interdisciplinary perspective on the diversity of older users, their social material and cultural circumstances, their needs and wishes, and their everyday practices of media (and) service use" (Sourbati 2008, p. 102). Following this suggestion by Sourbati, the present study draws upon the multiple frameworks applied in previous studies of practices of use of new technologies and upon social representations theory (Farr & Moscovici 1984) and focuses on ageing and social wellbeing. In particular, social representation (SR) theory has proven useful in conceptualising communities as facing and giving meaning to novelties through social construction processes. Thus, for us it is an ideal tool for analysing how elderly people socially construct the meaning of new technologies and for verifying if the social construction is connected with their perceived social wellbeing.

Social representation theory – among the different sociological perspectives that currently address the meaningfulness of the relation between technology and humans – particularly resonates with domestication theory and phenomenology.

Domestication theory describes the adoption and use of ICTs in four dimensions: appropriation, objectivation, integration and conversion (Silverstone 2006, Silverstone & Haddon 1996). Appropriation is the process that describes the flexible and changeable interaction between the human and the technological and that involves human agency. Objectivation is the practical process of placing the new technologies inside the home space by restructuring the micro-politics of gender and generation relationships and by reorganising the command over the domestic space. Integration is the process of injecting the practices of use of the new media into the rhythms, pauses and rituals of everyday life. Conversion is a process that involves display and the development of skills, competencies and literacies. These four processes suggest a reinterpretation of the non-adoption of new technologies as the results of digital choice rather than digital exclusion. Individuals, in fact, select technologies or some of their functions in their life according to their values, priorities and needs. One's own characteristics and socio cultural constraints, as well as social networks and significant others, are thus fundamental to understanding why individuals may or may not integrate a specific technology. The use of relational technologies, such as the telephone, may even increase on the part of retired elderly people who need to keep in touch with family members, relatives and friends. On the contrary, the potentialities offered by other technologies (e.g. Web 2.0) may not be recognised if individuals participate in peer relationships and networks that do not use these media (Haddon 2000).

As for phenomenology, this approach has been suggested as a way to address the integration of new technologies by looking at everyday experience and inter-subjective negotiations. From this perspective, Tsatsou (2011) recently analysed digital divides and their relationship to cultural differences in western and southern European countries. In a nutshell, results show the role that both policy and socio-cultural factors have played in shaping digital divides in Southern Europe. For example in Greece, it turned out that a lack of timely policies added to a generalised lack of interest towards the Internet, thus leading to "resistance" as a key driver in the interaction with it. In Portugal, instead, the effectiveness of policy efforts as regards Internet diffusion was obstructed by everyday life practices, conservative values and high levels of distrust towards the government.

While domestication theory and the phenomenological approach are among the most-applied theories to explain the practices of use of new technologies, research on social representations (SR) adds important dimensions to both. The analysis of integration of new technologies into the household context is expanded by SR beyond individual experience to the socio-cognitive level. SR studies, in fact, address the relationship between system and meta-system, that is the interface between individual meanings and systems of normative regulation as they are developed in the public sphere (Fortunati 2009). Moreover, although SR and phenomenology share the same ontology, SR theory puts more emphasis on the social and communicative dimension rather than on direct experience. As Tsatsou (2011) also recognised, individual agency should be contextualised and historically traced. SR theory addresses this point and suggests looking at the continuous, situated reconstruction of meanings that happens in contemporary societies rather than at inherited and long-lasting cultural constraints.

For these specificities, the process of domestication and integration in everyday life has been investigated in SR research by exploring how these technologies were socially elaborated and shared with the purpose of constructing a common understanding (Contarello & Fortunati 2006, Contarello & Sarrica 2007, Fortunati & Manganelli 2008).

The application of SR theory will enable us to analyse the social construction of the new technologies elaborated by the elderly, to verify if this representation by the elderly is connected to their perceived wellbeing. In this way we will be able to reinforce the criticism of the cited assumptions regarding elderly people. The present chapter is structured as follows.

In the next section, available statistical data on the diffusion of new technologies and the practices of their use among the elderly in Italy is reported. The SR approach is then introduced and discussed, as is the notion of wellbeing. In the next section the study conducted by the authors among a sample of elderly individuals living in two rural communities in southern Italy is presented and the data illustrated in respect to their social consequences. The final discussion presents the main results and indicates directions for further research. In the concluding remarks we come back to the theme of the inclusion of the elderly through new technologies and we highlight our critical observations.

The diffusion of new technologies in Italy

A detailed picture of the diffusion of new technologies in Italy is provided by a national survey on citizens and new technologies conducted yearly by the Italian Institute of Statistics (ISTAT 2010, 2012). The statistical report indicates that Italy is behind many European countries in regards to access to the Internet and the quality of infrastructure. Only 59% of households have access to the Internet and only 49% have a broadband connection. The mobile phone is broadly diffused among elderly families.

Age and place of residence are two main factors which influence the diffusion of new technologies. In Italy, as in many other countries (Commission of the European Communities 2007, Rogers et al. 2005), the elderly use the Internet and mobile phones less, on average, than does the broader population (Ling 2008). A significant gap can be observed between families composed only of individuals over 65 years of age and other families, especially those with at least one underage component. A second significant gap (stable at around 10%) is observed in Italy between families living in northern and southern Italy. Families living in the North own more technological devices and more often have a broadband connection than families living in the South. Data concerning the possession of mobile phones showed a less significant yet persistent gap between northern (90.4%) and southern families (86.3%) in 2010. In 2012, while the mobile is diffused in almost all the families (92%), differences are observed as regards Internet-connected mobiles and smartphones.

The trend of ICT diffusion over the last five years, however, shows a general increase and has been explained by the ageing of baby boomers into old age (Adler 2006, Blaschke et al. 2009, Czaja & Lee 2003); in other words, it has been explained more in terms of generations than of cohorts (Colombo & Fortunati 2011).

When asked about their reasons for not using the Internet, 55.7% of elderly households refer to a lack of capability. A significant number of these families, however, declare that they do not use the Internet because it is not useful for them, and thus they are not interested in it (28.0%). Italians aged 65–74 and over 75, on the contrary, tend to use the Internet at rates similar to or even over the national average for very specific tasks, such as: looking for health information, online banking, phone calls and video calls, all functions that are of particular interest to them.

These results extracted from the ISTAT survey on new technologies (2010, 2012) seem to support the two premises discussed in the introduction – that is, that the elderly lack cognitive capabilities and the abilities to use these new technologies. The results in question cohere with the general trend observed in North America and in other European countries (Rogers et al. 2005, Blaschke et al. 2009), and emphasise some factors which explain the lack of use of new technologies among the elderly: habits, rewards and attitudes. Emotion has recently been indicated to be a fourth important factor. Let us review them briefly.

1. Habits. Research has indicated that the speed of diffusion of various types of technologies might be explained by looking at the pressure that their general diffusion provokes in the population (Rogers 1995). It is evident that the spread of a specific device among the population makes it progressively more necessary to learn how to use it, as can be observed in the case of the mobile phone in Italy.

2. Costs and rewards. The elderly, as with other age groups, attribute benefits to the various devices and adopt criteria in order to weigh the costs and rewards connected with the use of each technology. Costs, in the case of the elderly, include both the cognitive efforts needed to acquire the new skills required to use new devices as well as the expenses associated with buying and maintaining said devices (Blaschke et al. 2009). In general, rewards such as communication opportunities have proven to be fundamental to the decision to accept new technologies; this has been observed regardless of age.

3. Attitudes. According to Rogers, Stronge and Fisk (2005), "Age related differences in attitudes towards technology have been assessed in a number of studies. In many cases, relative to younger adults, older adults reportedly had more strongly negative attitudes, for example, about computers" (p. 140). Furthermore, positive interactions with technology and the accrual of experience tend to rapidly improve attitudes towards them. One reason for such a reaction is the reduction of anxiety that occurs in these cases. And anxiety is one of the most relevant emotional states acting to mediate individuals' attitudes toward computers (Ellis & Allaire 1999).

4. Emotion. Renewed interest has been devoted to the role of emotion in the relationship with ICTs (Vincent & Fortunati 2009). First, ICTs are objects of emotions. The mobile phone in particular has become more and more an extension of the human body (Fortunati 2003, Fortunati et al. 2003) and an object of such an intense degree of attachment as to render it a veritable part of personal identity. Second, new technologies convey users' emotion

and also provoke emotion with their mediatised content, in addition to contributing to the development of new languages and modes of communication online (Baron 2010).

5. Finally, the use or non-use of different devices elicits various emotional states that also affect the problematic issue of trust in computer-mediated communication (Dunn & Schweitzer 2005, Gergen 2003). Research carried out in five European countries including Italy (Fortunati & Manganelli 1998) indicates that the intense use of ICTs in general is significantly associated with positive emotions such as joy, relaxation and feelings of accompaniment. More ambivalent emotions are linked to mobile phones: due to their capacity to bring perpetual contact, mobile phones are both a source of intimacy and form of symbolic attachment (Vincent 2005) as well as a source of discomfort and anxiety in the public sphere (Beckers et al. 2008).

Social representations and new technologies in Italy

Surveys on ICTs often monitor the diffusion of devices and may implicitly suggest that new technologies act as unique forces on individuals and communities which have the choice only of using or rejecting them (Fortunati 2010). Many scholars have shown, on the contrary, that new technologies are characterised by a structural ambivalence and that the "two opposing fronts – those in favour of technology and those against – are understandable if we take into account that technology is situated in the realm of novelties." (Fortunati & Vincent 2009, p. 6). Opposed perspectives document uncertainty and opacity associated with the digital era and processes of resistance towards new technologies (Bauer 1997), of their appropriation (Boczkowski 2004, Boczkowski & Ferris 2005) and domestication (Silverstone 2006).

From a socio-psychological perspective, the SR approach (Moscovici 1961/1976) provides a comprehensive framework within which researchers can examine how communities make sense of and define what technological novelties are and how they are related to daily life. A social representation is defined as a "socially elaborated and shared form of knowledge that has a practical goal and builds a reality that is common to a social set" (Jodelet 1989, p. 48).

Social representations are emotionally loaded sets of knowledge that emerge when communities have to cope with novelties (see Jovchelovitch 2007) that are characterised by structural ambivalence and rapid diffusion. The unfamiliar is first associated with previous knowledge through anchoring, then it is transformed into "an icon, metaphor or trope, which comes to stand for the new phenomenon" (Wagner et al. 1999, p. 99).

From these premises, a series of studies has been carried out in Italy on the social representation of new technologies. Such studies have aimed at exploring symbolic and emotional features linked with ICTs and at monitoring the relationship among different practices (Contarello & Fortunati 2006, Contarello et al. 2007, Contarello et al. 2008, Contarello & Sarrica 2007, Fortunati & Contarello 2002, Fortunati & Manganelli 2008, Sarrica et al. 2010). From an early date, these authors included in their research an exploration of wellbeing among the same groups of respondents. From this wave of inquiries the key finding has been that the representation of the Internet has come to be governed by a basic dichotomy. On the one hand, "the Net" was represented as a boundless space that elicited frightening and/or challenging experiences. On the other hand, it was represented as a concrete and delimited place in which to meet friends. This second pole of the representation, first observed several years ago, prefigured a possible shift towards a more intimate use of the Web, compared to when it was undertaken mainly by young adults. Interestingly, the debate on the fragmentation of the Internet (see, for example, *The Economist*, Sept 2, 2010) is coherent with this trend, as users increasingly adopt applications which allow the sharing of information within a restricted circle of acquaintances.

Another finding that has emerged from this set of studies is that the representation of the mobile phone has from the start been multifaceted, since it merged functional, identity-related contents, emotional investments and negative evaluations. The analysis of its evolution during the last decade reveals, for example, that the mobile phone was first equated to the "old telephone" for its communicative functions, then became an attractive-but-dangerous object at the beginning of 2000 (e.g. it was associated with health concerns), to go back more recently to functional descriptions (Contarello et al. 2007).

Ageing, wellbeing and new technologies

This stream of research on the social representations of the new technologies has recently intersected with studies on ageing and on the issue of emotion and social wellbeing (as devised by Keyes 1998) in the late stages of life.

Several theoretical perspectives on "ageing and wellbeing" in the socio-psychological domain question the assumption that ageing necessarily means a decrease in the quality of life and in the sphere of social relationships. Research has shown that a great variety of attitudes and behaviours occurs depending on individual strategies of coping with "becoming older" and on social strategies of constructing "being older".

In particular, the Socioemotional Selectivity Theory (Carstensen 1991, 1993) suggests that a change in the relative salience of emotional needs occurs during life. More specifically: "As people age, they realise that time, in a sense, is "running out", and begin to focus on the present as opposed to the future... subsequently... they care more about experiencing emotional ties and less about expanding their horizons" (Carstensen et al. 2003, p. 107). Similarly, the Successful Ageing perspective (Baltes & Baltes 1990) argues that the elderly are able to adopt efficient coping strategies that are based on three processes:

1. selection of competences and actions compatible with biological constraints;

2. optimisation of previous skills to learn new abilities; and,

3. compensation for decay with remaining abilities or/and with help from the outside.

Finally, a more radical proposal has been put forth by Kenneth and Mary Gergen (2000, 2002) in their advocacy for Positive Ageing. The authors deconstruct the biological and cultural dimensions of ageing and argue that "there is no process of ageing in itself; the discourse of ageing is born from interpersonal relationships within a given culture at a given time" (Gergen & Gergen 2002, p. X).

Various investigations on this topic have reaffirmed the importance of taking into account social construction processes when defining ageing.

Investigations conducted in Italy confirm that emotional wellbeing does not decrease with age, especially among active elderly people who maintain a large social network (Gasparini et al. 2011) and support the distinction between physical decay and ageing (Gastaldi & Contarello 2006). Cultural differences have also been recognised in this regard (Contarello et al. 2011).

Further research examining the connection of social representations of ICTs with the issues of ageing and wellbeing (Contarello et al. 2011) has shown that elderly people conceptualise the Internet as a source of progress, characterised by usefulness and fullness of information; however, critical aspects, such as complexity and perceived menace (down to "taboo subjects") are also associated, especially by those over 75 years of age. Secondly, elderly respondents conceptualise the mobile phone in positive and pragmatic terms, as they consider it useful and convenient, especially in cases of emergency. Critical aspects are not lacking, however; they relate especially to annoyance and violation of privacy caused by the mobile phone. The general view on new technologies, however, is positive. These results are in line with the idea that generativity and openness do not necessarily decrease with age but, on the contrary, may be maintained or even increase. Elderly respondents reported a slight increase in social wellbeing after the advent of the Internet and the entrance of the mobile phone into their everyday life, especially as it related to the dimensions of actualisation and coherence – that is, the perception that the world is quickly evolving and that they were still able to understand its organisation and functioning. Social integration, contribution and acceptance also increased significantly for the elderly, yet less than other dimensions such as being part of the community, contributing to it and being open to novelties, all of which were augmented by new technologies, although to a lesser extent than actualisation and coherence.

The above-mentioned studies were conducted with convenience samples of elderly individuals living mainly in the north of Italy and they do not claim to be generalisable. They have been shown to be useful, however, in questioning some of the tropes that popular rhetoric on the digital divide had considered untouchable. The present study builds on this wave of studies and investigates the relation between ageing, wellbeing and new technologies, as they are experienced by the elderly living in southern Italy, a context that very few have so far explored.

The Research

Aims

As discussed above, the primary aim of the present study is to investigate how elderly people socially construct the meaning of new technologies and how this social construct is related to their perceived social wellbeing. Building on the theoretical and empirical framework outlined above, we operationalised our broad scope by exploring the social representations of the Internet and the mobile phone shared by elderly people living in rural communities in southern Italy. In particular, we were interested in investigating the shared contents and the organising principles of their representations and in deepening our understanding of the emotions connected to new technologies. Secondly, we were interested in exploring how these social constructions are anchored to self-reported social wellbeing.

Participants

The participants were a convenience sample of 100 elderly people (men N = 45; women N = 55) living in small-and-medium-sized villages (with inhabitants less than 2,000 and 37,000, respectively) in the region of Puglia in southern Italy. Particular attention was devoted to the age range of potential users, as we considered separately three age levels close to those which the literature on ageing has so far referred to as the young elderly (65–69, N= 55), the elderly (70–74, N= 25), and the old or oldest old (over 75, N= 20).[3]

Research design, materials and procedure

The research design benefited from previous studies conducted on social representations and on the practices of use of new technologies, as well as from the research on ageing and wellbeing that we mentioned above.

The main tool was a questionnaire which included several sections designed to explore the different components of social representation of new technologies: information, attitude and representation (Le Bouedec 1984), as well as experienced social wellbeing, and its relationship with new technologies.

First, the information component and the representational field were investigated through a free association task: participants were asked to write the first five words that came to their mind when they thought of the following stimuli: the Internet, the mobile phone and elderly people using ICTs.

Second, respondents' social wellbeing was monitored: given that social wellbeing was seen as a significant component of overall wellbeing, along with emotional and psychological wellbeing, an adapted version of the scale developed by Keyes (1998) was employed here. Hence in the second section of the questionnaire, a short version of the scale (22 items instead of 33) measured social integration, acceptance, contribution, actualisation and coherence.

Practices of use and personal information were collected in the third section of the questionnaire. This section included questions on ownership, level of familiarity with the Internet and the mobile phone, reasons for using them, frequency of use and places of access to the devices, as well as gender, age, education and socio-economic status.

---

[3]   These definitions have already been adjusted again by demographers (Tebano 2013), following the increase in life expectancy. For example, now the elderly have been split into young elderly (65–75), elderly (76–84) and old elderly (over 85).

In the fourth section, respondents were asked to rate whether and to what extent each of the five areas of social wellbeing had improved or worsened after the advent of the Internet and the mobile phone.

In the final section, we explored the emotions related to new technologies, asking respondents to describe the emotions they felt when using new technologies. The questionnaires were administered by two independent researchers. Participants were randomly contacted from among the elderly people of the villages and, once we had obtained their agreement to participate, they were met in a familiar context (e.g., at home, in the bar). The questionnaire was self-administered, but the researchers supported the participants and explained the tasks when necessary.

Data analysis

Free associations were analysed with the help of the SPAD package. The textual corpora were pre-treated to reduce synonyms and to fix typos, and the inclusion frequency threshold was defined. The aim of the pre-treatment was to reduce the dispersion of data and to identify relevant categories of contents. In this sense, the choice to reduce synonyms to a single form and to identify a threshold reduces individual variability and the nuances of expressions while stressing shared semantic categories.

The resulting matrix of associated terms provided by respondents was submitted to a correspondence factor analysis in order to identify the representational field and its organising principles. Correspondence factor analysis (CFA) is based on the chi square metric and is suitable for categorical data; CFA aims at reducing the information present in a large matrix of data to a space with few dimensions. Similar to principal component analysis, it allows the detection of underlying dimensions (i.e. factors) that organise the relationships between active categorical variables. These dimensions can be eventually depicted as the axis of a Cartesian plane. Results of CFA can be enriched by illustrative variables: these are categorical variables usually associated with respondents that do not contribute to identifying the axis, however it is possible to estimate their coordinate on each of the dimensions emerging from the analysis of active variables. Illustrative variables can thus be projected on the plane in order to show, for each dimension, the positioning of different categories of respondents (Greenacre & Blasius 1994). This technique is usually adopted in exploratory research on SR, especially to explore data collected through free associations tasks because it allows researchers to detect the relationships between semantic categories, the dimension that organises these relationships (representational field) and to suggest the position taken by groups of respondents, that is the anchoring of the representation to psychological, psycho-social and sociological variables.

In this study, data concerning social wellbeing, ownership and use of the Internet and of mobile phones were entered as illustrative variables in order to examine the anchoring of the social representations (for more details on the method employed here, see Contarello & Sarrica 2007).

Results

As regards social wellbeing (Table 2.1), four of the five dimensions of the scale show fair or good reliability (Cronbach's alpha > .65). The measure of actualisation was not reliable (alpha = .49) and was hence excluded from further analyses.

One sample t-test on composite scores showed that the mean scores were significantly different from the centre points of the response scales. Participants reported relatively high levels of perceived contribution and good levels of integration and coherence. Acceptance – that is, the degree of openness toward the generalised other – was shown to decrease to levels below the median value. No differences were observed between men and women or among the young elderly (65–69), the elderly (70–74) and the oldest old (over 75).

Table 2.1. Social wellbeing

	Mean	SD	Cronbach's alpha
Contribution	3.88**	.67	.69
Acceptance	2.75*	.68	.71
Integration	4.09**	.55	.68
Coherence	3.35**	.92	.65

Note: One sample t-test, significant differences from the median point (3) of the scale: * $p < .05$; ** $p < .01$

The Internet

The vast majority of respondents (86%) declared that they did not use the Internet. This means that the following findings illustrate a vision of the Internet expressed largely by people who do not use it. Accordingly, only a few reported using it for communication (e.g., email, online calls, forums, chat services, etc.), to search for information (e.g., to browse or to surf the Web) or for other functions (e.g., buying and selling, peer-to-peer exchanges). The most frequent reason advanced for non-use was a lack of interest (43%), followed by a lack of capability ("would not know how to use it" 34%) and, much more rarely, by a lack of information ("never heard about it", "don't know where I could use it" 3%). In this respect it is worth noting that the lack of interest is even higher than the national average (ISTAT 2010) (43% vs. 28%), while the lack of capability is lower (34% vs. 55.7%).

Analysing the content of the representation as illustrated by the free associations task (total distinct words: 28; total words: 289), the Internet emerges as a source of pitfalls but also of useful information and communication, including wide-ranging contacts (global information highways) as well as learning, progress and work (Table 2.2).

Table 2.2. Content of the representations
of the Internet: Most frequent terms
evoked by the stimulus "Internet"

Terms evoked	Frequency
Pitfalls	26
Useful	23
Good	21
Information	20
Computer	19
Sky	15
World	14
Contact	13
Learning	12
I'm not interested	12
Communication	12
Progress	11
Work	10
Information highways	9
I like it	9
Good and bad things	8
Total	234

The representation field – the result of correspondence analysis performed on the matrix of 28 words by 100 participants – appears somehow meagre, with very few images and a high presence of evaluations and references to the self (e.g., "I like it", "I don't use it", etc.; Table 2.3).

The first factor can be defined as *good but not for me* vs. *the social world at home*. This factor opposes a potentially positive evaluation intertwined with a distant stance to the idea of a new form of communication both rich and concentrated in a single personal place (Table 2.3). The first view is mostly held by respondents who reported feeling highly integrated in their community, but was shared by those who felt they contribute less to society and find it more difficult to understand. The second polarity was held mainly by participants with a lower degree of social integration.

Table 2.3. The Internet: Correspondence factor analysis

1st Fact.	Terms	Coordinate	Abs. contrib.	Terms	Coordinate	Abs. contrib.
Inertia 7.09%	Good but not for me			The social world at home		
	I don't understand it	-4.46	58.30	Everything-at-home	1.46	4.19
	Good	-0.89	8.05	Contacts	0.77	3.72
				Communication	0.79	3.61
	Female: High integration; Low contribution; Low coherence			Male: Low integration		
2nd Fact.	Terms	Coordinate	Abs. contrib.	Terms	Coordinate	Abs. contrib.
Inertia 6.87%	Acknowledgement without understanding			Progress and potential menaces		
	I don't understand it	-2.53	19.31	Pitfalls	1.23	19.74
	Everything-at-home	-1.69	5.74	I'm not interested	1.44	12.57
	Communication	-0.95	5.47	Convenient	1.69	5.75
				Stress	2.25	5.10
				Good and bad things	1.07	4.59
				Progress	0.81	3.63
	Male			Female: High integration; Low acceptance; Negative emotion; Do not use		

The second factor can be defined as *acknowledgement without understanding* vs. *progress and potential menaces*. On the one hand, this second factor combines the two poles of the first; on the other, it expresses a clearly ambivalent view in which convenience and progress are combined with potential menaces (e.g., "pitfalls", "stress", etc.) and kept at a distance (e.g., "I am not interested"). Again, this latter, ambivalent view was mostly expressed by respondents who reported feeling well integrated in their social context, but also by those who expressed a lower degree of trust in people (lower acceptance), who endorsed negative emotions towards the technology and who did not use it. As to gender, women gave voice mainly to the ambivalent position (first pole of the first factor, second pole of the second), while men mostly underlined the communicative strength of the device.

Despite this dry and ambivalent representation, the general view on the Internet in relation to social wellbeing is far from negative. Participants report that all the dimensions of their social wellbeing increased after the advent of the Internet.[4]

Mobile phones

The results concerning mobile phones differ quite markedly. A vast majority of respondents (81%) reported owning a mobile, using it often to speak (48%) or for urgencies and emergencies (42%), but rarely to text (10%).

Table 2.4. Content of the representations of the Mobile phone: Most frequent terms evoked by the stimulus "Mobile phone"

Terms evoked	Frequency
Useful	44
Comfort	22
Feel close to the ones I miss	19
Accident/emergency	17
Messages	17
Lovely	16
Availability	16
Communication	15
Indispensable	12
I don't like it	8
Boosters	8
Accessible to everyone	8
Total	202

---

[4] Participants were asked to rate their wellbeing after the advent of the Internet on a five-point scale ranging from 1 (far less than before) to 5 (much more than before). Mean and Standard Deviations are respectively: Contribution M= 3.25**, SD=.63; Acceptance M=3.15*, SD=.70; Integration M=3.18**, SD=.52; Coherence M=3.47**, SD=.77. One sample t-test showed significant differences from the median point (3 = as much as before) of the scale: * p <.05; ** p <.01.

Table 2.5. The mobile phone: Correspondence factor analysis

1st Fact.	Terms	Coordinate	Abs. contrib.	Terms	Coordinate	Abs. contrib.
Inertia 5.74%	*Useful but dangerous substitute*			*Infrastructure for a speedy communication*		
	Substitute-fixed-telephone	-3.28	10.78	Boosters	3.19	40.83
	Useful	-0.42	3.85	Answer-and-call	2.03	10.28
	Bad-use-adolescents	-1.37	3.77	Messages	0.83	5.83
	I don't like it	-0.91	3.31	Speed	1.53	3.52
	Female: Mobile phone use; High integration			**Over 75; Male: Do not use the mobile phone**		
2nd Fact.	Terms	Coordinate	Abs. contrib.	Terms	Coordinate	Abs. contrib.
Inertia 5.57%	*Dislike*			*Substitute for the landline and infrastructure*		
	I don't like it	-0.86	3.06	Substitute-fixed-telephone	8.71	78.22
				Boosters	0.91	3.44
	High contribution			**Low contribution**		
3rd Fact.	Terms	Coordinate	Abs. contrib.	Terms	Coordinate	Abs. contrib.
Inertia 5.21%	*Ephemeral and emergency use*			*Easy, intimate and misused communication*		
	I don't use it	-2.72	20.35	Bad-use-adolescents	1.71	6.43
	Indispensable	-1.64	17.86	Easy communication	1.39	6.35
	Not owned before	-1.34	5.93	Answer-and-call	1.41	5.50
	Accident/emergency	-0.72	4.81	Feel-close-those-I-miss	0.64	4.35
	Used indiscriminately	0.90	3.12	Boosters	0.83	3.03
	Low acceptance					

Analysing the content of the representation resulting from the free associations task (total distinct words: 34; total words: 287), we found a very positive and pragmatic view of the device as a source of usefulness, comfort, help in cases of emergency and closeness to loved ones (Table 2.4). The negative side of the device manifests only rarely, evidenced in terms such as annoyance (frequency = 7), indiscriminate use (freq = 7) and a strict aversion (e.g., "I don't like it", freq = 8).

The representation field, however – from correspondence factor analysis performed on the matrix of 34 words by 100 participants – brings to the forefront elements of ambivalence and concern (Table 2.5).

We have interpreted the first factor as *a useful but dangerous substitute for the landline* vs. *infrastructure for speedy communication*. Again, reported social wellbeing enters into the picture, showing that higher social integration is mostly linked with the ambivalent view of the technology emerging from the first pole of the factor (e.g., where the mobile is seen as useful, but also badly abused by teenagers and overall not liked by the respondents). This viewpoint was particularly common among women while men, taking up a position on the second pole of the factor, mostly described the functions of the mobile (e.g., calls, texts, etc.), its speed and, most importantly, the boost it provides to all communication exchanges.

The second factor is particularly bare and we interpreted it as *substitute for the landline and infrastructure* vs. *dislike*. It sets the idea of the mobile phone as a replacement of the landline made possible by boosters against a straightforward negative evaluation: "I don't like it". These two polarities reintroduce a prior distinction made between description and evaluation. In line with the above-mentioned results regarding the Internet, this refusal came mostly from respondents with high levels of social wellbeing, in particular those who feel they make a greater contribution within their own community.

Ambivalence again permeates the third factor, which we propose to encompass *ephemeral and emergency use* vs. *easy, intimate and misused communication*. On the first pole, acknowledgement of necessity – particularly for urgencies and emergencies – goes hand in hand with criticisms (e.g., "indiscriminately use") and personal distance (e.g., "I do not use it"), while on the second pole fruitful and easy forms of communication (e.g., "easy communication", "call and answer", "feeling close to distant ones", etc.) are associated together with boosters and misuse by teenagers. Again, social wellbeing plays a role: participants who show less trust in people (lower levels of social acceptance) and (with a statistical trend) those who feel themselves to be less integrated in their social context express a double-faceted position linked with a sharp declaration of non-use.

Overall, the general views regarding the mobile phone in relation to social wellbeing were positive. Among respondents, social wellbeing after the introduction of the mobile phone appears to have improved in everyday life, not dramatically but significantly.[5] Only acceptance – that is, openness to the generalised other – has not improved, thus supporting the use of this means of communication within the restricted circle of relatives and acquaintances.

Discussion

In order to shed light on the discourse about the digital divide within the debate on age, generation and new technologies, this study has sought to combine different traditions and methods of research. In particular, we have explored the social representations of the Internet and the mobile phone shared by elderly people, and relationships with perceived social wellbeing. The match of these different strands of research (social representation and wellbeing) proved to be very effective in shedding new light on the theme of social inclusion.

First, our results support indications that ageing does not necessarily mean exclusion or marginalisation. On the contrary, our sample of elderly individuals reported generally high levels of satisfaction with the quality of their role within society (Social Integration). They perceive themselves to be vital members of their community (Social Contribution), and they perceive good quality of organisation and functioning within their community (Social Coherence). On the other hand, they showed little trust in others (Social Acceptance).

As mentioned, our participants live in rural areas of southern Italy – that is, a context characterised by relatively low diffusion of the Internet and a relatively high level of diffusion of mobile phones. The generation of the elderly investigated here were late adults in the moment of diffusion of new technologies and were living thus only partially exposed to the use of these technologies.

The data generated in this study has thus far highlighted several points. The social representations of the Internet and the mobile phone outlined by our convenience sample of elderly people are ambivalent but more positive than negative and mirror the meanings underlying the process of domestication of these two technologies. The Internet gives them the opportunity to bring the social world home and enrich their level of

---

5   Participants were asked to rate their wellbeing after the advent of the mobile phone on a five-point scale ranging from 1 (far less than before) to 5 (much more than before). Mean and Standard Deviations are respectively: Contribution M=3.57**, SD=.73; Acceptance M=3.14, SD=.74; Integration M=3.24**, SD=.64; Coherence M=3.33**, SD=.68. One sample t-test showed significant differences from the median point (3 = as much as before) of the scale: ** $p < .01$.

information, knowledge and entertainment, while the mobile phone enables them to communicate immediately even on the move. Yet reservations and criticism are also associated with these technologies.

These results recall the ambivalence reported in analogous investigations on social representations of ICTs carried out in the second half of the 1990s, and are in line with more recent findings (Contarello et al. 2011).

As regards wellbeing, the reported contribution to society on the part of these elderly respondents is quite positive on the whole, although some caveats must be raised.

Both the devices inquired about seemed to enhance comprehension and mastering of the world (the Internet more so than the mobile phone) as well as the possibility of making an active contribution to society (the mobile phone more so than the Internet).

Reported social wellbeing was nevertheless not automatically connected with the use and appreciation of new technologies. From the first factor of the correspondence analysis regarding the Internet, those who are more socially integrated say that the Internet is good but not for them and, in the second factor, they consider it uninteresting, although they perceive it as a sign of progress combined with a potential menace. Findings from the correspondence analysis regarding the mobile phone moreover show that those who dislike this device are those who are more socially integrated and those who feel themselves more able to make a greater contribution to society.

We can carry this line of interpretation still further by saying that reported social wellbeing is more likely to be connected to an ambivalent attitude toward the mobile phone and the Internet. As regards the mobile phone, lesser degrees of social integration and social acceptance are associated with the ephemeral and emergency use of this device. As regards the Internet, a greater degree of integration is connected with not using this technology and with resultantly ambivalent attitudes toward it.

These findings are very important because they suggest that these two technologies are not automatically perceived by the elderly as enhancing their degree of social inclusion. These results seem in a way opposed to those by Tsatsou (2011), who showed that especially in southern European countries openness to the other and towards societal change were associated with use of the Internet. However, it shall be noticed that our research was carried out in two small/medium villages, where perceived integration and contribution might be associated with shared conservative values and with currently no need for mediated communication. We may thus hypothesise that the ambivalence of the social representation of the new technologies signals a conflict between societal pressure and habits developed with acquaintances: whereas society asks for new practices of use, it is especially the close circles that continue to be relevant to the wellbeing of elderly people. Those feeling more integrated and having stronger ties with the close communities also feel that they do not need to use the new devices.

In the end, the correspondence analysis yielded an unexpected result: the idea that the Internet allows new forms of communication both rich and concentrated in a single, personal place – that is, "everything-at-home". This metaphor is interesting because it goes back to the basic dichotomy that has governed the social representation of the Internet as a boundless or a delimited place (Contarello & Sarrica 2007). The first pole of this dichotomy, that also characterised a number of previous studies on the Internet and the telephone, asserts that the Internet and both the fixed-line and the mobile telephone have emerged in these investigations as windows which open out to the wider world, symbolising the primary function of these devices – their capacity to overcome the walls of the home and to open up the possibility of contact with (and the chance of being contacted by) the world. In the present study the other side of the coin is perceived by elderly people. The Internet is not conceived of as a way to open the house door and go into the world, it is rather is a tool that brings the world into the home, within the domestic sphere. It could be useful to enrich domestic life, but maybe not for our respondents, who prefer to invite friends and relatives to their home.

This representation stresses the communicative function over knowledge expansion, with an implicit control over communications: communication is understood in fact with already established contacts, it is a relational function much more than an informational function. This approach seems to be coherent with the fragmentation that currently characterises the Internet and its intimate use. The findings drawn from our convenience sample of elderly people endorse this view of the Internet, and this result is coherent with the Socioemotional Selectivity Theory (Carstensen 1991, 1993), which has suggested that the elderly care more about experiencing emotional ties and less about expanding their horizons.

The representation of the mobile phone lacks metaphors and is more centred on functional features. In particular, the results show that this device is strongly conceptualised as a substitute for the fixed-line telephone. This idea is very vivid, as it grasps a strong tendency in Italy where the broad diffusion of the mobile phone tends to undermine that of the fixed telephone (Fortunati & Manganelli 2011).

The age groups taken into account here – the young elderly, the elderly and the oldest old – do not differ consistently or significantly as pertains to representations of these technologies (including their contents, attitudes and practices). Future research will need to continue to differentiate between age cohorts and generations in order to understand the meaning of this apparent lack of differentiation. This result, but in general the whole picture offered in this study, invites further investigation into the current impact of ageing and age cohorts – particularly with the entrance of post-war generations into ageing – on the wellbeing and on the representations and practices of use of new technologies. Gender is instead seen as a more significant anchoring variable. Specifically, women take a more active stance toward the mobile phone and less so toward the Internet, as the second factor of the correspondence analysis shows. On the contrary, men limit themselves to depicting the technical and functional features, especially of the mobile phone, but are more distant than are women from their material use. Elderly women – who seem to be more fully integrated than their elderly male counterparts – appear to be more sensitive to the problems that the disruptive consequences of the use of these technologies can cause. Given the exploratory nature of the present study, further investigations are still needed. To produce a clear and meaningful picture of the relationship between the elderly and new technologies future investigations will need to use a representative sample of the investigated population. Larger samples from different contexts may contribute to efforts to evaluate the specificities and commonalities of the social representations detected in this study, with representations emerging from other research cohorts and/or from other Italian contexts. In this regard the results of the current investigation are coherent with those of previous studies (Contarello & Fortunati 2006, Contarello et al. 2007, Contarello et al. 2008, Contarello & Sarrica 2007, Fortunati & Manganelli 2008, Sarrica et al. 2010), but, again, they are not at all generalisable.

In summary, our results show that the relationship the elderly have with new technologies is far more complex than the debate on the digital divide has envisaged up to now.

Concluding remarks

The present study was prompted by a critical perspective on two of the premises which often shape investigations on the elderly and new technologies: first, that new technologies could enhance the social inclusion of the elderly and hence that the elderly should approach new technologies in the same way as do younger people; and second, that the elderly suffer a digital divide because of their lack of interest and capacities. The results of the current research are not generalisable, however they are consistent with other studies carried out with different samples (e.g. Contarello et al. 2011). In particular, the first of these two premises on social inclusion, which assumes that the role of new technologies would be positive by definition, should be critically revisited. The second – the purported lack of interest and capacity on the part of the elderly – is empirically supported by the results of the present study for the Internet but not for the mobile phone. Thus we conclude that it is not possible to generically talk of the elderly's deficiency in relation to new technologies: elderly people evaluate each new technology according to their needs and goals and, consequently, they develop different attitudes towards each new technology. Furthermore, the different diffusion of these two technologies is one more proof that digital technologies are not all equal, but some are inclusive (mobile phone) while others are exclusionary (Internet).

What is more important is that the elderly are often criticised for this lack of interest and demonstrated capacity without an attempt to understand to what extent this lack of interest and capability is created by the social system. Attempts to enhance the use of new media among elderly people with the aim of increasing their wellbeing may fail if they continue to be influenced by the rhetoric surrounding the topic and if they do not recognise the proactive role that the elderly play in defining what new technologies are and what they could be, which functions they enable and which functions they would need, and if and how they represent a menace or a positive contribution to their perceived social wellbeing.

References

Adler, R. (2006). *Older Americans, Broadband and the Future of the Net.* (Online).

Baltes, P.B., & Baltes, M.M. (Eds.) (1993). *Successful Aging: Perspectives from the Behavioral Sciences* (Vol. 4). Cambridge: Cambridge University Press.

Baron, N. (2008). *Always on: Language in an Online and Mobile World.* Oxford: Oxford University Press.

Bauer, M. (Ed.) (1997). *Resistance to New Technology: Nuclear Power, Information Technology and Biotechnology.* Cambridge: Cambridge University Press.

Beckers, J., Schmidt, H., & Wichers, J. (2008). Computer anxiety in daily life: Old history? In E. Mante-Maijer, L. Haddon & E. Loos (Eds.), *The Social Dynamics of Information and Communication Technology* (pp. 13–24). Aldershot Hampshire (UK): Ashgate.

Blaschke, C.M., Freddolino, P.P., & Mullen, E.E. (2009). Ageing and technology: A review of the research literature. *British Journal of Social Work, 39*(4), 641–656.

Boczkowski, P.J. (2004). *Digitizing the News: Innovation in Online Newspapers.* Cambridge, MA: MIT Press.

Boczkowski, P.J., & Ferris, J.A. (2005). Multiple media, convergent processes, and divergent products: Organizational innovation in digital media production at a European firm. *The Annals of the American Academy of Political and Social Science, 597*(1), 32–47.

Carstensen, L.L. (1991). Selectivity theory: Social activity in life-span context. *Annual Review of Gerontology and Geriatrics, 11,* 195–217.

Carstensen, L.L. (1993). Motivation for social contact across the life span: A theory of socioemotional selectivity. In J.E. Jacobs (Ed.). *Nebraska Symposium on Motivation: 1992, Developmental Perspectives on Motivation, 40* (pp. 209–254). Lincoln: University of Nebraska Press.

Carstensen, L.L., Fung, H.H., & Charles, S.T. (2003). Socioemotional selectivity theory and the regulation of emotion in the second half of life. *Motivation and Emotion, 27*(2), 103–123.

Colombo, F., & Fortunati, L. (2011). *Broadband Society and Generational Changes.* Frankfurt am Main: Peter Lang.

Commission of the European Communities (EU) 2007. *Ageing Well in the Information Society.* (Online).

Contarello, A., Bonetto, R., Romaioli, D., & Wachelke, J. (2011). Invecchiamento e intercultura. In G. Leone (Ed.). *Vivere l'interculturalità. Ricerche sulla Vita Quotidiana* (pp. 171–182). Milano: Unicopli.

Contarello, A., & Fortunati, L. (2006). ICTs and the human body: A social representation approach. In P. Law, L. Fortunati & S. Yang. (Eds.), *New Technologies in Global Societies* (pp. 51–74). Singapore: World Scientific Publishing

Contarello, A., Fortunati, L., Gomez Fernandez, P., Mante-Meijer, E., Vershinskaya, O., & Volovici, D. (2008). ICTs and the human body: An empirical study in five countries. In E. Mante-Maijer, L. Haddon & E. Loos, (Eds.), *The Social Dynamics of Information and Communication Technology* (pp. 25–38). Aldershot Hampshire (UK): Ashgate.

Contarello, A., Fortunati, L., & Sarrica, M. (2007). Social thinking and the mobile phone: A study of social change with the diffusion of mobile phones, using a social representations framework. *Continuum: Journal of Media & Cultural Studies, 21*(2), 149–163.

Contarello, A., & Sarrica, M. (2007). ICTs, social thinking and subjective well-being: The Internet and its representations in everyday life. *Computers in Human Behavior, 23*(2), 1016–1032.

Contarello, A., Sarrica, M., & Romaioli, D. (2011). Ageing in a broadband society. An exploration on ICTs, emotional experience and social well-being within a social representation perspective. In F. Colombo & Fortunati L. (Eds.), *Broadband Society and Generational Changes* (pp. 247–258). Oxford: Peter Lang.

Czaja, S., & Lee, C. (2003). The impact of the Internet on older adults. In N. Charness & Schaie, K.W. (Eds.), *Impact of Technology on Successful Aging* (pp. 113–133). New York: Springer Publishing.

Dunn, J.R., & Schweitzer, M. E. (2005). Feeling and believing: The influence of emotion on trust. *Journal of Personality and Social Psychology, 88*(5), 736–748.

Ellis, R.D., & Allaire, J. (1999). Modeling computer interest in older adults: The role of age, education, computer knowledge, and computer anxiety. *Human Factors, 41,* 345–355.

Farr, R., & Moscovici, S. (Eds.) (1984). *Social Representations.* Cambridge: University Press.

Fortunati, L. (2003). The human body: Natural and artificial technology. In J. Katz (Ed.), *Machines that Become Us* (pp. 71–87). New Brunswick (N.J.): Transactions.

Fortunati, L. (2009). Theories without heart. In A. Esposito & R. Vich (Eds.), *Cross-Modal Analysis of Speech, Gestures, Gaze and Facial Expressions* (pp. 5–17), Berlin: Springer.

Fortunati, L. (2010). Afterword: De-structuring the meaning of the mobile Phone. *Encyclopaideia, Journal of Phenomenology and Education, XIV*(28), 155–175.

Fortunati, L., & Contarello, A. (2002). Internet-mobile convergence: via similarity or complementarity? *Trends in Communication, 9,* 81–98.

Fortunati, L., Katz, J., & Riccini, R. (Eds.) (2003). *Mediating the Human Body: Technologies, Communication and Fashion.* Mahwah (N.J.): Lawrence Erlbaum Associates.

Fortunati, L., & Manganelli, A.M. (1998). La comunicazione tecnologica: comportamenti, opinioni ed emozioni degli europei'. In L. Fortunati (Ed.), *Telecomunicando in Europa* (pp. 125–194). Milano: Angeli.

Fortunati, L., & Manganelli, A.M. (2008). The social representation of telecommunications. *Personal and Ubiquitous Computing, 12,* 421–431.

Fortunati, L., & Manganelli, A.M. (2011). Social participation and mobile communication. In J. Katz (Ed.), *Machines that Become us* (pp. 273–290). New Brunswick (N.J.): Transaction Publishers.

Fortunati, L., & Vincent, J. (2009). Introduction. In J. Vincent & L. Fortunati (Eds.), *Electronic Emotion. The Mediation of Emotion via Information and Communication Technologies.* Oxford: Peter Lang.

Gasparini, G., Sarrica, M., & Contarello, A. (2011). Processi di regolazione emotiva e benessere emotivo nell'invecchiamento. Uno studio sul modello della socioemotional selectivity theory di Carstensen. *Ricerche di Psicologia, 1,* 63–85.

Gastaldi, A., & Contarello, A. (2006). Una questione di età. *Ricerche di Psicologia, 4,* 7–22.

Gergen, M., & Gergen, K.J. (2002). Positive aging: New images for a new age. In J. F. Gubrium & J. A. Holstein (Eds.), *Ways of Aging* (pp. 203–224). Oxford: Blackwell.

Gergen, K.J. (2003). Self and community and the new floating worlds. In K. Nyri (Ed.), *Mobile Democracy: Essays on Society, Self, and Politics* (pp. 103–114). Wien: Passagen Verlag.

Gergen, K.J., & Gergen, M. (2000). *The New Aging: Self Construction and Social Values.* (Online).

Greenacre, M., & Blasius, J. (1994). *Correspondence Analysis in the Social Sciences.* London: Academic Press.

Haddon, L. (2000). Social exclusion and information and communications technologies: Lessons from studies of single parents and the young elderly. *New Media and Society, 2,* 387–406.

ISTAT (2010). *Cittadini e Nuove Tecnologie.* (Online).

ISTAT (2012). *Cittadini e Nuove Tecnologie.* (Online).

Jodelet, D. (1989). *Folies et Représentations Sociales.* Paris: PUF.

Jovchelovitch, S. (2007). *Knowledge in Context. Representations, Community and Culture.* London: Routledge.

Keyes, C.L.M. (1998). Social well-being. *Social Psychology Quarterly, 61*(2), 121–140.

Le Bouedec, G. (1984). Contribution à la methodologie d'étude des representations sociales. *Cahiers de Psychologie Cognitive, 4*(3), 245–272.

Ling, R. (2008). Should we be concerned that the elderly don't text? *The Information Society, 24*(5), 334–341.

Moscovici, S. (1961/1976). *La Psychanalise, Son Image, Son Public.* Paris: PUF.

Rogers, E.M. (1995). *Diffusion of Innovation.* New York: Free Press

Rogers, W.A., Stronge, A.J., & Fisk, A.D. (2005). Technology and aging. *Reviews of Human Factors and Ergonomics, 1*(1), 130–171.

Sarrica, M., Grimaldi, F., & Nencini, A. (2010). Social representations of citizenship and multimedia use practices: An exploratory research with young people. *Revue Internationale de Psychologie Sociale, 23,* 37–62.

Silverstone, R. (2006). Domesticating domestication: Reflections on the life of a concept. In T. Berker, M. Hartmann, Y. Punie & K.J. Ward (Eds.), *The Domestication of Media and Technology* (pp. 229–248). Maidenhead: Open University Press.

Silverstone, R., & Haddon, L. (1996). Design and the domestication of information and communication technologies: Technical change and everyday life. In R. Mansell & R. Silverstone (Eds.), *Communication by Design: The Politics of Information and Communication Technologies* (pp. 44–74). Oxford: Oxford University Press.

Sourbati M. (2008). On older people, Internet access and electronic service delivery: A study of sheltered homes. In E. Mante-Maijer, L. Haddon & E. Loos (Eds.), *The Social Dynamics of Information and Communication Technology* (pp. 95–104). Aldershot Hampshire (UK): Ashgate.

Stevenson, S. (2009). Digital divide: A discursive move away from the real inequities. *The Information Society*, *25*(1), 1–22.

Tebano, E. (2013, March 29). Le nuove (mezze) stagioni della vita. *Corriere della Sera*, 31.

The Economist, (2010, September 2). The future of the Internet. A virtual counter-revolution. *The Economist*. Retrieved from http://www.economist.com/node/16941635.

Tsatsou, P. (2011). *Digital Divides in Europe: Culture, Politics and the Western-Southern Divide*. Oxford: Peter Lang.

Vincent, J. (2005). Emotional attachment to mobile phones: An extraordinary relationship. In L. Hamill, & A. Lasen (Eds.), *Mobile World: Past, Present and Future* (pp. 93–104). London: Springer Verlag.

Vincent, J., & Fortunati, L. (Eds.) 2009. *Electronic Emotion. The Mediation of Emotion via Information and Communication Technologies*. Oxford: Peter Lang.

Wagner, W., Duveen, G., Farr, R., Jovchelovitch, S., Lorenzi-Cioldi, F., Marková, I., & Rose, D. (1999). Theory and method of social representations. *Asian Journal of Social Psychology*, *2*, 95–125.

Chapter 3

STUDYING CRISIS COMMUNICATION ON SOCIAL MEDIA

Conceptual patterns and methodological concerns

Francesca Comunello

The aim of this chapter is to build a conceptual framework for analysing the role of social media in major crises, with special regard to emergency response, from a scholarly research point of view. Existing literature has hitherto addressed the topic aiming at contributing both to public policies in emergency situations and to scholarly research. Social media have served as a powerful tool for emergency disaster management in many recent emergency situations, particularly natural disasters, including Hurricane Katrina in the U.S. and the Queensland floods in Australia, to major earthquakes worldwide. The huge number of messages and interactions generated on social media during emergencies, moreover, constitute an unprecedented source for understanding the specific communication patterns taking place on social media, with regard to information spread and influence dynamics. After introducing the perspective of Internet Studies on technology mediated communication and social media, we analyse the role of social media in emergency response, mainly focusing on information spread dynamics, on the perspective of emergency services and institutions, and on citizens' activities beyond information spread. We conclude by providing some conceptual and methodological remarks.[1]

Introducing crisis communication and social media from an Internet Studies perspective

Internet Studies is a multidisciplinary field – or a *meta-field* (Silver 2004) – of studies that deals with the relations between contemporary society and digital

---

[1]   A discussion on overall crisis communication issues goes beyond the scope of this chapter; for an extensive approach to crisis communication, see Coombs 2007.

technologies (for a first *Handbook of Internet Studies,* see Consalvo & Ess 2011); while mainly relying on conceptual frameworks and empirical methods originating from the social sciences and the humanities, they also integrate more technology-focused disciplines, such as information science and network science. Wellman (2004, 2011) identified "three ages" of Internet Studies: the first went from 1995 to 1998, the second from 1998 to 2003; and the third age of Internet Studies (2004 to today), introduced a shift from documentation to analysis, emphasising the role of empirical research in order to understand better the way the Internet is integrated into people's lives, and focusing on the relations between the online and the offline world.

The broader conceptual framework we adopt for understanding the communicative and relational role of digital media relies on a wide range of theories covering digital technology, social relations, and participatory cultures (Jenkins et al. 2009), with a main focus on Wellman's and Castells' understanding of Networked Individualism and Networked Sociability.

> The culture of individualism does not lead to isolation, but it changes the patterns of sociability in terms of increasingly selective and self-directed contacts. [...] The critical matter is not technology, but the development of networks of sociability based on choice and affinity, breaking the organizational and spatial boundaries of relationships [...]. Networked sociability leads both to an individual-centred network, specific to the individual, and to peer-group formation, when the network becomes the context of behavior for its participants. (Castells et al. 2007, pp. 143–144).

In the last few years, social media – and especially Social Network Sites (SNS) – have constituted a major research topic for Internet scholars, not only because of their growing popularity among Internet users worldwide, but also because they represent "powerful playgrounds, both for the user and for the researcher" (Comunello 2011, p. xix).

For social scientists, SNS represent environments where identity and relational performances can be observed; these are, on the one side, deeply embedded into people's everyday lives and strongly connected to their face-to-face sociability and, on the other side, "publicly articulated" (boyd 2004), visible, more persistent and, therefore, easier to analyse.

According to the work of boyd and Ellison, SNS can be defined as Web-based services that allow individuals to:

- Construct a public or semi-public profile within a bounded system;
- Articulate a list of other users with whom they share a connection;

- View and traverse their list of connections and those made by others within the system.

The nature and nomenclature of these connections may vary from site to site. (boyd & Ellison 2007)

While this chapter addresses the overall social media environment, our main focus will be SNS, as identified by the above-mentioned definition (and therefore including, among others, the *microblogging* platform Twitter). SNS are not only the most mentioned platform in social media and crisis communication literature, they also appear as one the most effective social media environments for information spread and emergency management.

Early research on SNS has mainly focussed on identity performances and on relational patterns, and the consideration of privacy issues (and the so-called "privacy paradox", Barnes 2006). For instance, identity performances in SNS have been commonly related to personal profile shaping, underlying people's awareness in self-presentation practices (Rybas & Gajjala 2007, boyd 2008, Livingstone 2008), and *impression management* processes (Ellison et al. 2006); a major role has been attributed to profile pictures and personal photographs (among others, Sessions 2009, Mallan & Giardina 2009). With regard to relational patterns, some scholars have focused on the strength of online ties (Boase et al. 2006), others have analysed friending strategies and the related social negotiation practices (boyd & Heer 2006), and others still have underlined the consequences of SNS use on the overall structure of social relations (Ito et al. 2008, Lee 2009, Lewis & West 2009). The vast majority of SNS studies in the first decade of the 21st century has focused on Facebook, which is the most popular – and least-*specialised* – platform.

More recently, SNS have started to become "mainstream sites of relational maintenance" (Baym 2010, p. 134), showing a seamless integration into people's everyday relational patterns. While SNS use is being *normalised*, research on SNS has started to become more specialised. While relational and identity-based topics are still an important part of SNS scholarship, a growing amount of research is being devoted to the practices of applying SNS to more specialised fields, such as civic engagement, political participation, public administration, branding and consumption, and so on (Comunello 2011, p. xxi; for an insightful account on advanced SNS research, see Papacharissi 2011). Moreover, the ever-evolving technological environment requires scholars to devote their attention to a variety of different platforms and to specific usage practices.

The study of crisis communication on social media certainly belongs to such a specialised wave, not only because it focuses on specific and specialised communication and information practices, but also because its peculiarities require consideration of a variety of platforms, ranging from Twitter to more experimental ones, such as geosocial networking systems.

Analysing the role of social media in emergency response

Research on the role of social media during "acute events" (Burgess & Crawford 2011) has both focused on natural disasters and on "human-made crises" (Bruns et al. 2012), such as the so-called "Arab Spring". In this chapter, we will mainly focus on natural disasters, as the role of social media in "human-made crises" appears to be strongly biased by ideological concerns regarding the supposed revolutionary role of social media. Literature on the "Arab Spring", for instance, shows a deep polarisation between techno-enthusiasts and techno-sceptics, who overemphasise – or completely mini-mise – the role of digital communication in Arab uprisings (see, for instance, the debate between Gladwell 2010 and Shirky 2011, also in Gladwell & Shirky 2011; for an analysis of the debate between *digital evangelists* and *techno-realists* vis-à-vis Arab uprisings, see Comunello & Anzera 2012).

Social media and crisis communication from the perspective of emergency services and institutions

Research on the role of social media during natural disasters has been oriented towards both practical work (for instance, proposing emergency management guidelines addressing emergency services and media organisations), and pure scholarly research. While such approaches often need to be kept separate for analytical purposes, our understanding of the role of social media during natural disasters from both practical and scholarly research perspectives would surely benefit from a stronger integration between practical and theoretical work.

In the last couple of years, several authors have published work on the use of social media in crisis communication and emergency management, offering practical guidelines to emergency services and policy makers. White (2012), for instance, provides a comprehensive analysis of SNS, with a main focus on Facebook and Twitter proposing several case studies that show their effectiveness in emergency situations; the author analyses the peculiarities of different digital platforms, suggests precise design strategies and underlines the role of social media both in institutional information spread and in citizen engagement, focusing on collaborative "community resilience" and participatory tools and practices. Crowe (2012) analyses social media policy and procedures in emergency contexts, also focusing on the role of *crowdsourcing*[2] and citizen engagement (considering as well the role of "citizen journalism"); this work also underlines the potential of social media monitoring and the role of specific innovative applications and usage practices, such as location-based social media, multimedia content, mobile and emerging platforms.

From a purely research perspective, scholars have focused on public institutions and emergency services activities, and on citizen response to emergencies. Some scholars, moreover, have succeeded in proposing results that explicitly address both emergency services and citizens' responses (Bruns et al. 2012).

Research has recently shown that digital media are strongly affecting public administration. Their impact is evident in administrative procedures, data management, the functioning and delivering of public services and, moreover, the communication between public organisations and citizens (Contini & Lanzara 2009). There is also a general request for a new phase of transparency, openness and participation (Sirianni 2009), where citizens can have an active role in stimulating innovative practices of communication and dialogue (Lovari & Parisi 2011). In this scenario, social media and in particular SNS play an important role in re-defining relationships, power dynamics and communication strategies between institutions and citizens (Castells 2009, Dahlgren 2009).

According to Nabatchi and Mergel (2010), social media can increase citizen involvement in public sector policies and decision-making processes. At the same time, Lindmark (2009) reports that through using Web 2.0 tools citizens can play an active role at different levels in the delivery of public services; for example, they can become content providers, test applications in a perpetual beta process, or contribute to developing innovative services.

Information spread dynamics during "acute events"

Scholars have analysed the role of SNS in emergency contexts, both focusing on users' activities and institutional communication for information spread and disaster relief. For instance, Cheong and Lee (2011) underline the role of

---

[2]   "Crowdsourcing is the practice of obtaining needed services, ideas, or content by soliciting contributions from a large group of people, and especially from an online community, rather than from traditional employees or suppliers" (http://en.wikipedia. org/wiki/Crowdsourcing, 24 February 2013).

Twitter monitoring in analysing civilian sentiment and response to terrorist attacks, proposing a framework for harvesting civilian sentiment on Twitter and creating a knowledge base to be used by decision makers for effective response. When analysing the 2011 Australian Queensland floods, Burns et al. (2012) focus both on the overall Twitter dataset on the topic and on the specific activity of an institutional account – @QPSmedia, the official account of Queensland Police Service – underlining its role as a source of information, as a tool for coordinating help and fundraising activities, and for false rumour management (through a specific hashtag, #Mythbuster). Mendoza et al. (2010) have also focused on rumour management, in that case user reactions to rumours on Twitter during the 2010 earthquake in Chile, showing that false rumours tend to be more questioned by Twitter users than confirmed truths.

Rumour management is strongly related to the broader issue of information spread in social media, a topic that has been addressed by a number of scholars. While the structure of Facebook and its prevailing usage practices tend to rely mainly on pre-existing networks (someone's "friends" and, to some extent, "friends of friends"), Twitter provides an asymmetric relational environment (based on "following" and "followers", without the need for reciprocity); the majority of Facebook users tend to have private or semi-private accounts, and to "follow" ("like", in Facebook terms) a relatively limited number of institutional pages. Twitter users, in comparison, tend to have public accounts. Moreover, some specific Twitter features, such as the RT (retweet) feature, that allows users to forward a tweet (with or without any further comment) to their followers, and the relevance of the "public" dimension of #hashtag conversations, make Twitter a more suitable platform for information spread (and for information spread analysis). While significant forms of information circulation are to be found also on Facebook, its nature makes it more difficult, for public institutions, emergency operators and single citizens to rely on Facebook to spread relevant crisis information on a real-time basis. Jansen et al. (2009) carried out an early study on Twitter as a form of electronic word of mouth, with a main focus on customer opinion concerning brands; Wu et al. (2011) analysed a large dataset, in order to understand information production, flow and consumption on Twitter; and boyd et al. (2010) analysed the motivations and the practices of retweeting, showing how it can generate conversational practices.

Another important topic in information spread on social media is the role of so-called influencers, people who have the power to exert a relevant influence on a large number of social media users. Scholars and market operators have dedicated some effort to identifying influencers, but there is currently no commonly accepted definition of the concept. Empirical evidence from large datasets shows that while users who have been influential in the past and who have a larger number of followers are more likely to be influential in the future, it is hard to formulate specific predictions of influence patterns (Bakshy et al. 2011). Kwak et al. (2010) have analysed Twitter structure and information flow, showing, for instance, that there is no clear direct correlation between the number of followers and the number of retweets. Cha et al. (2010) agree, showing that top users, with regard to their "popularity" (users with a high "indegree"[3]), have little overlap with top users based on retweets (that represent "the content value of one's tweets") or mentions (that "represent the name value of a user"). They also underline that "most influential users hold significant influence over a variety of topics", while ordinary users "can gain influence by focusing on a single topic and posting creative and insightful tweets that are perceived as valuable by others" (ibid., p.11). Moreover, broadcast media accounts play a major role in influencing Twitter users.

Information spread is a particularly sensitive topic during emergencies: general information about the emergency situation itself, specific information on the conditions of individuals and information on emergency management and disaster relief (including coordinating help and fundraising) are crucial, and often hugely time-sensitive. Moreover, institutional sources need to find their way to become influential, in order to spread useful and verified information, and to limit the circulation of false rumours. Analysing the public flow of tweets related to a violent crisis in the Seattle-Tacoma area (USA), Heverin and Zach (2010) found that Twitter was mainly a method of sharing crisis related information, underlining the significant number of retweets. When considering the "original tweet/retweet ratio", Twitter datasets regarding emergencies tend to show a disproportionately high level of retweets, underlining user willingness to share the breaking news. Bruns et al. (2011), for instance, have found that users showed a particularly high tendency to amplify information by retweeting during the early days of the Queensland floods. Analysing the earthquake in Emilia, Italy, on 20 May, 2012, Boccia et al. (2012) noted a prevalence of original tweets with hashtag #terremoto (=earthquake) in the very early hours of the first shake (4.00–6.00 am local time), while the ratio changed during the second shake (3.00

---

[3]   In a directed network (a network where ties have directions) "indegree" is a count of the number of ties directed to the node (see http://en.wikipedia.org/wiki/Centrality).

pm–5.00 pm local time). Nevertheless, original tweets prevailed during the first 30 minutes of each major shake: in the early minutes, the "witnessing" function prevails over the "information amplification" function, which starts prevailing afterwards. Bruns et al. (2011) have noted that the role of retweets tends to lessen slightly by the time broadcast media and institutional Twitter accounts start covering the event. Several studies, moreover, have shown that during emergencies users are more likely to include URLs in their tweets (Hughes & Palen 2009, Heverin & Zach 2010, Bruns et al. 2012), therefore demonstrating a willingness to spread larger amounts of inform-ation, consistent with a *convergence culture* approach (Jenkins 2006), using Twitter as a tool that is embedded in a broader multimedia information en-vironment (with a prevalence of image and video sharing, Bruns et al. 2012, pp. 33–36). According to Starbird and Palen (2010), messages by broad-cast media accounts are more likely to be retweeted, and local media and emergency operators are perceived as particularly valuable sources.

In comparison to what happened during the Queensland floods, there was no institutional Twitter emergency management activity during the Italian 2012 earthquake, with the sole relevant exception of the account @INGVterremoti.[4] Direct witnesses and influential users, followed by broadcast media and other corporate accounts, contributed to spreading the news.

Citizen activities beyond information spread

In the early stages of any emergency, citizens use social media as a tool for receiving and spreading information, often anticipating traditional broadcast media. Grassroots information, or citizen journalism, plays a major role in covering areas that cannot be immediately covered by broadcast media. In the subsequent stages, however, social media are commonly used for a variety of purposes: Bruns et al. (2012) found that during Queensland floods, in addition to information distribution (both sharing original tweets and other media content), users generated tweets related to help and fundraising activities, reporting direct experience, and offering reactions and discussion. In the early stages, there was a prevalence of information sharing, while in subsequent stages a major role was played by reactions and discussion; tweets directly mentioning the official Queensland Police Service account show a neat prevalence of informative content. In a longer temporal perspective,

---

[4]   INGV (Istituto Nazionale di Geofisica e Vulcanologia) is the National Institute for Geophysics and Vulcanology; its experimental account provides verified information on an earthquake's magnitude and other seismic information.

moreover, social media are often used for mourning and grieving, for sharing memories, and for citizen activism and mobilisation (see the chapter by Farinosi and Tréré in this volume). Lev-On (2012) studied how a community of Israeli evacuees used a variety of media to keep in touch, express opinions and maintain a sense of community, even from long distance, adopting a uses and gratifications approach. His results show the diversity and multiplicity of media people rely on to pursue their goals (including mobile phones and face-to-face interactions). Liu (2010) underlines the role of social media in building collective memories and what she defines as "grassroots heritage" in crisis contexts, proposing a "grassroots heritage framework" for facilitating "collaborative curation". Starbird and Palen (2011) analyse self-organising practices carried out on Twitter by "digital volunteers" after the 2010 Haiti earthquake. They focus on the production and motivations of "crisis tweeters", contributing to better understanding of the broad concept of crowdsourcing, and underlining the enabling role of Twitter in volunteering even from long distance. Bruns (2011) also focuses on grassroots activities, underlining the role of social media in fostering ad-hoc communities and forms of self-organisation that are crucial for dealing with rapidly developing events, such as natural disasters, and also connecting such phenomena to the concept of e-democracy. In case of "acute events", citizens may also need to find ways to express their emotions. Carroll and Landry (2010), for instance, have studied how young people use SNS (with a main focus on MySpace and Facebook) for grieving and mourning.

While the study of the activities of emergency operators and citizen reactions to major crisis can be kept separated for analytical purposes, integration between the two spheres is crucial for effective crisis management. As claimed by Palen et al. (2010) in their programmatic research, self-organising citizens should be actively involved in emergency response activities, without considering them a mere audience for institutional messages; a stronger dialogue between institutions and citizens, based on high transparency levels, can be enabled by an effective use of social media.

This scenario has been further extended by the rise of location-based media, the diffusion of mobile social networks (e.g. Gowalla, Foursquare) and the release of location based versions of well-known online applications (e.g. different Google products, Facebook, Twitter etc.). Through these tools people can easily publish comments, suggestions, reviews, photos and videos and then visualise these contents as embedded in digital maps. By means of a process of "social annotation" users produce a large amount of information referring to different places and then share it with other users.

Mobile social networks and geo-local services are crucial in emergency situations, not only because the mobile Internet provides connectivity virtually everywhere (sometimes constituting the sole connection to the outside world, when landline telephones are out of service), but also because geo-referred information is essential in many stages of emergency management. Among other participatory usages, a platform like Ushahidi,[5] for instance, and its interactive mapping and information gathering services, has been successfully used in responding to different crises, as, for instance, the 2010 Haiti earthquake (Morrow et al. 2011). Moreover, geocoded tweets can help seismologists gather useful data for augmenting "earthquake response products and the delivery of hazard information" (Guy et al. 2010), thus improving earthquake response (Earle et al. 2010).

In the following paragraphs, we provide some conceptual and methodological remarks that we believe can contribute to a better understanding of the role of social media in emergency response.

Some conceptual remarks

As we have seen, research on social media and crisis communication is strongly multidisciplinary: computer scientists and social scientists have hitherto played a major role in analysing the role of social media in emergency response. Furthermore, other scholars, such as seismologists, are also turning to social media in order to gather useful insights on such topics. Internet studies is an inherently multidisciplinary field, and its tradition of integrating social sciences approaches with computer science approaches can offer relevant resources for a better understanding of the role of social media in emergencies. Surely, therefore, further empirical research has to be carried out. Moreover, some conceptual patterns emerging from Internet Studies' understanding of the interactions between communication, social relations and digital technologies can help in developing a deeper understanding of the subject.

First of all, scholars investigating the role of social media in emergency response should abandon any technologically deterministic approach. Technological determinism is a perspective that assumes that technology shapes society. Similarly, early commentators mainly focused on the *consequences* of the Internet on social systems, disregarding the complex interactions between technology and social factors, the different contexts in which technologies can be used, the specific purposes people use technology

---

5   http://www.ushahidi.com/.

for – in Baym's words, without considering "what people do with mediated communication" (Baym 2010, p. 59). Accordingly, a rise in social media use in emergency response is not enough to grant better emergency management processes, if social media use is not integrated in broader communication and social processes. When addressing the role of social media in emergency response, scholars should acknowledge that digital technologies are not separated from people's everyday lives, and analysis should consider their integration into a multiple set of communicative environments (both mediated and non-mediated).

Furthermore, existing literature on social media and crisis communication, as well as broader literature on technology-mediated social relations – and especially SNS – has mainly adopted a platform-centric approach. For a better understanding of technology-supported social relations and communicative practices, however, an accurate knowledge of specific platforms should be integrated with an *ecological* perspective (Jenkins et al. 2009), considering the whole variety of tools and platforms that are used by individuals. As Rainie and Wellman point out:

> Networked individuals [...] use a panoply of gadgets and applications to orchestrate their lives. Theirs is a complicated dance through the networked operating system. They use email for certain kinds of networked communication; text messaging, Facebook posts, private Facebook messages, and Twitter posts for others; and phone calls for communication that requires more extensive conversation. (Rainie & Wellman 2012, p. 146)

Digital technologies can be understood as environments that offer specific affordances: people develop specific usage patterns both by taking advantage of such affordances and by further shaping this architecture (boyd 2011). Our culture has been defined as a *convergence culture*: a culture "where old and new media collide, where grassroots and corporate media intersect, where the power of the media producer and the power of the media consumer interact in unpredictable ways" (Jenkins 2006, pp. 259–60). For a better understanding of the rich communication environment people are relying on in emergency situations, we need an accurate knowledge of each platform's peculiarities (its affordances, its prevailing usage practices), and a broader ecological approach, considering the wide variety of environments (both on- and offline) people turn to in order to get information, advice, or a sense of community. For instance, the abovementioned evidence from social media and crisis communication research has highlighted widespread practices of multimedia sharing on Twitter. Even so-called "old media" can be at least partially involved in such processes. If we focus on information spread, for instance, grassroots media and broadcast media (or even institutional communication) should not be considered as completely separated. As Jenkins points out: "[t]he power of the grassroots media is that it diversifies; the power of broadcast media is that it amplifies. That's why we should be concerned with the flow between the two" (ibid., p. 268).

Some scholars suggest that the participatory practices related to convergence culture are providing people with skills that could also be applied to civic engagement (Bennett 2008, Dahlgren 2009, Jenkins et al. 2009), and also, therefore, to emergency-related online activities. While this may be true for a growing part of the world's population, two major issues affect people's opportunities to participate effectively in the information society. So-called digital divides still affect large parts of the world's population. Moreover, formal access to technology is not enough: for digital technology to make a real difference, higher levels of digital (or new media) literacy are required (Jenkins et al. 2009, van Dijk & Van Deursen 2010, Livingstone & Helsper 2010).[6] Moreover, different platforms have different diffusion rates, even among Internet users. When analysing the role of social media in emergency response, we should not ignore that a large part of the world's population is not using the Internet, and that even Internet users often have low digital literacy levels – or low vocality – on the Internet; we should, therefore, focus on the peculiarities of the populations involved, and of the situations we are dealing with, without assuming to know, *ex ante*, which platform is best suited for each specific situation.

Some methodological remarks

Crisis communication on social media has been diffusely studied through the analysis of medium-scale or large datasets of social media postings. Bruns and Liang (2012) offer an accurate account of an effective Twitter data extraction tool (*yourTwapperkeeper*), and identify three broad areas of analysis of Twitter datasets: a) statistical analysis and activity metrics; b) social network analysis; c) content analysis. Further analytical strategies include qualitative analysis of tweets (Bruns et al. 2012). Although such areas explicitly refer to Twitter analysis, their overall approach can also be adapted to other datasets.

---

[6]   For a broader account of the relations between digital divides and digital literacy, see Comunello (2010).

- Automated data analysis and activity metrics have been largely used by computer scientists, but also by social scientists, aiming at studying large datasets and providing a statistical account of Twitter activity, including tweet volume over time, distribution of activity across users, distribution of user visibility etc.; geocoded information can also be processed likewise.

- Social network analysis has also been largely used for analysing large datasets, with the main goal of exploring information spread and patterns of influence on SNS. Bruns and Liang (2012) identify different broad approaches to the study of Twitter datasets in crisis communication: homogeneous networks (e.g. user-to-user networks, keyword co-occurrence networks) or heterogeneous or hybrid networks (user-and-URL networks, user-and-keyword networks etc.).

- Content analysis has also been widely used by researchers to give a quantitative account of the textual content of the tweets; even if the 140-character length of the tweets limits the scope of such analyses, researchers can gather relevant insights by studying word occurrence and co-occurrence and relating them to specific users or user groups, to specific practices (e.g. retweets), etc.

Automated or semi-automated techniques for analysing large datasets also include *sentiment analysis* of the views and opinions expressed by users on social media, which is mainly employed in market research (for a critical account on sentiment analysis, see Andò 2010).

Such automated quantitative approaches, especially when adopted by social scientists, raise the controversial issue of "big data": while offering unprecedented powerful tools for analysing huge amounts of data, and suggesting to the humanistic disciplines "to claim the status of quantitative science", decontextualised and non-theory-driven big data analysis, as well as its "claims for objectivity and accuracy" can be misleading for social researchers. As Burgess and Crawford (2011) suggest, numbers do not "speak for themselves": if we do not want to limit our research to descriptive statistics there is a need for relevant research questions and for broader theoretical frameworks in order to interpret big data usefully. Moreover, social media companies tend to progressively limit researchers' access to their data, generating what Burgess and Crawford (2011) define as "new digital divides".

Qualitative tweet (or social media posting) analysis can only be conducted by drawing a sample from large datasets, or by focusing on more limited datasets. Nevertheless, it can provide relevant results in relation to specific research questions (for a qualitative analysis of Twitter data, although not related to crisis communication, see Papacharissi 2012).

Integrating several methods can provide more complete – and significant – results; Bruns et al. (2011), for instance, have integrated automated data analysis with social network analysis and thematic coding activity, offering insightful results.

Moreover, for a better understanding of the way in which people deal with emergencies – and with related communication activities – more "traditional" social science research methods are surely helpful. Researchers should not only focus on specific platforms, but try and track the whole variety of communication activities of the user; in doing so, traditional methods, such as surveys and in-depth interviews, if selected according to specific research questions, can play a major role.

Concluding remarks

In this chapter, we have mainly focused on the use of social media in emergency response, with a main focus on natural disasters. A broader understanding of the role of digital communication in handling natural hazards, however, should consider a longer temporal perspective, including not only the use of social media during the emergency and in the next few days (which are the main topics we have focused on in this chapter), but also its use in *rest* periods, a topic that has hitherto received little attention. During rest periods, citizens should be trained to better understand and handle emergency situations, providing accurate and effective scientific communication, including communication of uncertainty and risk.

As we have seen throughout this chapter, broader Internet research can provide useful insights to researchers working on social media and crisis communication; at the same time, results from social media and crisis communication research can be relevant for a broader understanding of social media usage practices, and of the related social dynamics. Moreover, for a better understanding of emergency communication on social media, a broader multidisciplinary approach is needed, including not only Internet scholars and information scientists, but also the scientists who provide knowledge on the specific natural phenomena. Furthermore, we need a deeper dialogue between emergency services, policy makers and scholars: research results can offer relevant insights to stakeholders, while practical expertise can provide researchers with relevant case studies and with a more nuanced knowledge of the field. For instance, research can offer policy makers powerful insights on each platform's affordances and usage practices, on how to select the best platform for each specific context (including specific communication goals and targets), on effective communication strategies (both for each selected platform and in a cross-media perspective), on the integration between online and offline communication, on how to foster verified information spread, on how to analyse citizen response to emergencies, and on the best dialogue techniques with citizens and stakeholders.

Furthermore, we also need a deeper dialogue, both from a practical and from a research perspective, between top-down institutional approaches and bottom-up crowdsourced emergency response. From a methodological point of view, large datasets offer unprecedented opportunities for data mining and analysis, and have been broadly used to study the role of social media during emergencies. But to gain relevant results, research should always be driven by relevant research questions, and rely on relevant conceptual frameworks.

References

Andò, R. (2010). The challenge of audience research on Web 2.0: The possibilities, problems and perspectives of sentiment analysis. In F. Comunello (Ed.), *Networked Sociability and Individualism: Technology for Personal and Professional Relationships* (pp. 63–77). Hershey, PA: IGI Global.

Bakshy, E., Hofman, J.M., Mason, W.A., & Watts, D.J. (2011). Everyone's an influencer: Quantifying influence on twitter. Paper presented at the WSDM '11 Conference, Hong Kong, China.

Baym, N. (2010). *Personal Connections in the Digital Age*. Cambridge: Polity Press.

Bennett, W.L. (2008). *Civic Life Online: Learning how Digital Media can Engage Youth*. Cambridge, MA: MIT Press.

Boase, J., Horrigan, J.B., Wellman, B., & Rainie, L. (2006). The strength of Internet ties. *Pew Internet and American Life Project*. (Online).

Boccia Artieri, G., Giglietto, F., & Rossi, L. (2012). *#terremoto! l'uso di Twitter durante il terremoto tra testimonianza, propagazione e commento*. Social Network Studies Italia. (Online).

boyd, d. (2008). Why youth (heart) social network sites. In D. Buckingham (Ed.), *Youth, Identity, and Digital Media* (pp. 119–142). Cambridge, MA: MIT Press.

boyd, d. (2011). Social network sites as networked publics: Affordances, dynamics, and implications. In Z. Papacharissi (Ed.), *A Networked Self: Identity, Community, and Culture on Social Network Sites* (pp. 39–58). New York, NY: Routledge.

boyd, d., Golder, S., & Lotan, G. (2010). Tweet tweet retweet: Conversational aspects of retweeting on Twitter. *Proceedings of HICSS-42*, Kauai, USA. (Online).

boyd, d., & Ellison, N. (2007). Social network sites: Definition, history, and scholarship. *Journal of Computer-Mediated Communication, 13*(1), 210–230.

boyd, d., & Heer, J. (2006). Profiles as conversation: Networked identity performance on Friendster. Proceedings of the Hawaii International Conference on Social Systems-HICSS-39. (Online).

Bruns, A. (2011). Towards distributed citizen participation: Lessons from Wikileaks and the Queensland floods. In P. Parycek, M.J. Kripp & N. Edelmann (Eds.), *Proceedings of the International Conference for E-Democracy and Open Government* (pp. 35–52). Krems: Danube University.

Bruns, A., Burgess, J., Crawford, K., & Shaw, F. (2012). *#qldfloods and @qpsmedia: crisis communication on Twitter in the 2011 South East Queensland floods.* Brisbane: ARC Centre of Excellence for Creative Industries and Innovation.

Bruns, A., & Liang, Y.E. (2012). Tools and methods for capturing Twitter data during natural disasters. *First Monday, 17*(4). (Online).

Burgess, J., & Crawford, K. (2011). Social media and the theory of the acute event. Paper presented at Internet Research 12.0, Seattle, USA.

Carroll, B., & Landry, K. (2010). Logging on and letting out: Using online social networks to grieve and to mourn. *Bulletin of Science, Technology & Society, 30*(5), 341–349.

Castells, M. (2009). *Communication Power.* Oxford: Oxford University Press.

Castells, M., Fernández-Ardèvol, M., Linchuan Qiu, J., & Sey, A. (2007). *Mobile Communication and Society: A Global Perspective.* Cambridge, MA: MIT Press.

Cha, M., Haddadi, H., Benvenuto, F., & Gummadi, K. (2010). Measuring user influence in Twitter: The million follower fallacy. Proceedings of the Fourth International AAAI Conference on Weblogs and Social Media. (Online).

Cheong, M., & Lee, V. (2011). A microblogging-based approach to terrorism informatics: Exploration and chronicling civilian sentiment and response to terrorism events via Twitter. *Information Systems Frontiers, 13*(1), 45–59.

Comunello, F. (2010). From digital divide to multiple divides: Technology, society and new media skills. In Y.K. Dwivedi, E. Ferro, J.R. Gil-Garcia, & M.D. Williams (Eds.), *Overcoming Digital Divides: Constructing an Equitable and Competitive Information Society* (pp. 588–605). Hershey, PA: IGI Global.

Comunello, F. (Ed.). 2011. *Networked Sociability and Individualism: Technology for Personal and Professional Relationships.* Hershey, PA: IGI Global.

Comunello, F., & Anzera, G. (2012). Will the revolution be Tweeted? A conceptual framework for understanding the social media and the Arab Spring. *Islam and Christian–Muslim Relations, 23*(4), 453–470.

Consalvo, M., & Ess, C. (Eds.) (2011). *The Handbook of Internet Studies.* Chichester: Wiley-Blackwell.

Contini, F., & Lanzara, G.F. (2009). *ICT and Innovation in the Public Sector: European Studies in the Making of e-Government.* New York, NY: Palgrave Macmillan.

Coombs, W.T. (2007). *Ongoing Crisis Communication: Planning, Managing, and Responding.* London: Sage.

Crowe, A. (2012). *Disasters 2.0. The Application of Social Media Systems for Modern Emergency Management.* Boca Raton, FL: CRC Press.

Dahlgren, P. (2009). *Media and Political Engagement: Citizens, Communication and Democracy.* Cambridge: Cambridge University Press.

Earle, P., Guy, M., Buckmaster, R., Ostrum, C., Horvath, S., & Vaughan, A. (2010). OMG earthquake! Can Twitter improve earthquake response? *Seismological Research Letters, 81*(2), 246–251.

Ellison, N., Heino, R., & Gibbs, J. (2006). Managing impressions online: Self-presentation processes in the online dating environment. *Journal of Computer-Mediated Communication, 11*(2), 415–441.

Ferro, E., Dwivedi, Y.K., Gil-Garcia, J.R. & Williams, M.D. (Eds). 2010. *Overcoming Digital Divides: Constructing an Equitable and Competitive Information Society.* Hershey, PA: IGI Global.

Gladwell, M. (2010, October 4). Small change: Why the revolution will not be Tweeted. *The New Yorker*.

Gladwell, M., & Shirky, C. (2011). From innovation to revolution. Do social media make protests possible? *Foreign Affairs*, *90*(2), 153–154.

Guy, M., Earle, P., Ostrum, C., Gruchalla, K., & Horvath, S. (2010). Integration and dissemination of citizen reported and seismically derived earthquake information via social network technologies. *Advances in Intelligent Data Analysis*, IX, 42–53.

Heverin, T., & Zach, L. (2010). Microblogging for crisis communication: Examination of Twitter use in response to a 2009 violent crisis in the Seattle-Tacoma, Washington Area. Proceedings of the 7th International ISCRAM Conference, Seattle, USA. (Online).

Hughes, A.L., & Palen, L. (2009). Twitter adoption and use in mass convergence and emergency events. Proceedings of the 6th International ISCRAM Conference, Gothenburg, Sweden. (Online).

Ito, M., et al. (Eds.) (2010). *Hanging Out, Messing Around and Geeking Out: Kids Living and Learning with New Media*. Cambridge, MA: MIT Press.

Jansen, B.J., Zhang M., Sobel, K., & Chowdury, A. (2009). Twitter power: Tweets as electronic word of mouth. *Journal of the American Society for Information Science and Technology*, *60*(11), 2169–2188.

Jenkins, H. (2006). *Convergence Culture*. New York: New York University Press.

Jenkins, H., Clinton, K., Purushotma, R., Robison, A.J., & Weigel, M. (2009). *Confronting the Challenges of Participatory Culture: Media Education for the 21st Century*. Chicago, IL: MacArthur Foundation.

Lee, S.J. (2009). Online communication and adolescent social ties: Who benefits more from Internet use? *Journal of Computer-Mediated Communication*, *14*(3), 509–531.

Lewis, J., & West, A. (2009). Friending: London-based undergraduate experience on Facebook. *New Media and Society*, *11*(7), 1209–1229.

Liu, S.B. (2010). Grassroots heritage in the crisis context: A social media probes approach to studying heritage in a participatory age. Proceedings of CHI 2010, 10-15 April, 2010 Atlanta, USA. (Online).

Lindmark, S. (2009). Web 2.0: Where does Europe stand? *JRC European Commission*.

Livingstone, S. (2008). Taking risky opportunities in youthful content creation: teenagers' use of social networking sites for intimacy, privacy and self-expression. *New Media and Society*, *10*(3), 393–411.

Livingstone, S., & Helsper, E. (2010). Balancing opportunities and risks in teenagers' use of the Internet: The role of online skills and Internet self-efficacy. *New Media and Society*, *12*(2), 309–329.

Lovari A., & Parisi, L. (2011). Public administrations and citizens 2.0. Exploring digital public communication strategies and civic interaction within Italian municipality pages on Facebook. In F. Comunello (Ed.), *Networked Sociability and Individualism: Technology for Personal and Professional Relationships* (pp. 238–263). Hershey, PA: IGI Global.

Mallan, K., & Giardina, N. (2009). Wikidentities: Young people collaborating on virtual identities in social network sites. *First Monday*, *14*(6). (Online).

Mendoza, M., Poblete, B., & Castillo, C. (2010). Twitter under crisis. Can we trust what we retweet? Paper presented at the ACM. 1st Workshop on Social Media Analytics (SOMA '10), Washington, DC, USA.

Morrow, N., Mock, N., Papendi, A., & Kocmich, N. (2011). *Independent Evaluation of the Ushahidi Haiti Project*. DISI- Development Information Systems International Ushahidi Haiti Project.

Palen, L., Anderson, K.M., Mark, G., Martin, J., Sicker, D., Palmer, D., & Grunwald, D. (2010). A Vision for Technology-Mediated Support for Public Participation & Assistance in Mass Emergencies & Disasters. *Proceedings of ACM-BCS Visions of Computer Science*.

Papacharissi, Z. (Ed.). (2011). *A Networked Self. Identity, Community, and Culture on Social Network Sites*. New York, NY: Routledge.

Papacharissi, Z. (2012). Without you I'm nothing: Performances of the self on Twitter. *International Journal of Communication*, 6, 1989–2006.

Rainie, L., & Wellman, B. (2012). *Networked: The New Social Operating System*. Cambridge, MA: MIT Press.

Rybas, N., & Gajjala, R. (2007). Developing cyberethnographic research methods for understanding digitally mediated identities. *Forum Qualitative Sozialforschung/ Forum: Qualitative Social Research*, 8(3), art. 35.

Sessions, L. (2009). You looked better on Myspace: Deception and authenticity on Web 2.0. *First Monday*, 14(6). (Online).

Shirky, C. (2011). The political power of social media: Technology, the public sphere, and political change. *Foreign Affairs*, 90(1), 28–41.

Silver, David. (2004). Internet/cyberculture/digitalculture/newmedia/fill-in-the-blankstudies. *New Media and Society*, 6 (1): 55–64.

Sirianni, C. (2009). *Investing in Democracy: Engaging Citizens in Collaborative Governance*. Washington DC: Brookings Press.

Shklovski, I., Burke, M., Kiesler, S., & Kraut, R. (2010). Technology adoption and use in the aftermath of Hurricane Katrina in New Orleans. *American Behavioral Scientist*, 53(8), 1228–1246.

Starbird, K., & Palen, L. (2010). Pass it on? Retweeting in mass emergency. Proceedings of the 7th International ISCRAM Conference. Seattle, USA. (Online).

Starbird, K., & Palen, L. (2011). "Voluntweeters": Self-Organizing by Digital Volunteers in Times of Crisis. *Proceedings of CHI 2011, Vancouver, Canada*.

Van Dijk, J. (2005). *The Deepening Divide: Inequality in the Information Society*. Thousand Oaks, CA: Sage.

van Dijk, J. & Van Deursen, A., & (2010). Inequalities of digital skills and how to overcome them. In Y.K. Dwivedi, E. Ferro, J.R. Gil-Garcia & M.D. Williams (Eds.), *Overcoming Digital Divides: Constructing an Equitable and Competitive Information Society*. Hershey, PA: IGI Global.

Warschauer, M. (2003). *Technology and Social Inclusion: Rethinking the Digital Divide*. Cambridge, MA: MIT Press.

Wellman, B. (2004). The three ages of Internet studies. *New Media and Society*, 6(1), 55–64.

Wellman, B. (2011). Studying the Internet through the ages. In M. Consalvo, & C. Ess (Eds), *The Handbook of Internet Studies* (pp. 17–23). Chichester: Wiley-Blackwell.

White, C. (2011). *Social Media, Crisis Communication and Emergency Management: Leveraging Web 2.0 Technologies*. Boca Raton, FL: CRC Press.

Wu, S., Hofman, J.M., Mason, W.A., & Watts, D. (2011). Who says what to whom on Twitter? Paper presented at Conference WWW 2011, Hyderabad, India. (Online).

SOCIAL MOVEMENTS, SOCIAL MEDIA AND POST-DISASTER RESILIENCE

Towards an integrated system of local protest

Manuela Farinosi and Emiliano Treré

On 6 April 2009 an earthquake occurred in L'Aquila, a small city in the centre of Italy, causing the death of more than 300 people. This tragic event led to a prompt increase in the adoption and use of Internet technologies by local citizens who appropriated social media platforms in order to reconstruct online the offline spaces of socialisation which had been damaged or destroyed by the quake. A year after the tragedy, to protest against the Italian State's failure to remove the debris from the historical city centre, some citizens decided to flee into the streets with wheelbarrows and autonomously remove the rubble: a new movement later labelled as "The People of the Wheelbarrows" ("PoW") emerged. These activists aimed at involving the citizenship in the decision processes regarding L'Aquila's reconstruction, in contrast to the government's top-down strategies, and at making the public aware of the issue of the debris removal and the urgent need for the historical centre's re-opening and reconstruction. This paper explores the Internet-related practices of the actors of the PoW. Our findings highlight the existence of an integrated system of local protest characterised by a complex communication ecology based on crossovers between traditional media and multiple digital technologies, and articulated between the online and the offline dimensions.

Introduction

On 6 April 2009 at 3.32 a.m., an earthquake measuring 6.3Mw struck L'Aquila, a small city (around 73,000 inhabitants) in the centre of Italy. It represented Italy's worst earthquake in 30 years and the deadliest since the 1980 Irpinia tragedy. It caused significant damage not only to the medieval centre but also to several surrounding villages. More than 300 inhabitants of L'Aquila were killed, around 40,000 people were made homeless and approximately 10,000 were forced to abandon the city and were housed in hotels on the Adriatic coast.

For safety reasons, immediately after the earthquake, downtown L'Aquila was declared "zona rossa" (a red zone) and police forces and numerous barricades permitted access only to a small part of the historic centre, the traditional social, political and economic heart of the city. Most alleys and squares were closed off, blocking downtown access to people.

One year later, the situation had not changed substantially: most of the city centre was still under military control and access was denied to ordinary citizens. In February 2010, however, something happened: Italian mainstream media reported a phone tap between two entrepreneurs. One was telling the other how he laughed in his bed when he heard the news of the L'Aquila earthquake, thinking about the opportunities to profit financially from the rebuilding process. This recording was reported by several newspapers and online platforms and provoked strong indignation. The extreme cynicism of the entrepreneurs worked as a catalyst on people who were tired of unfulfilled promises of reconstruction and contributed to the construction of a collective identity. A few days after the recording was made public, citizens started to reclaim the city centre and to confront the police who blocked access to the off-limit zone.

The protest gathered momentum thanks to the word of mouth generated on Facebook: "Those who were not laughing in L'Aquila at 3.32" and on Sunday 21 February, the annihilated downtown area became the stage of the first citizen protest called "Protesta delle 1,000 chiavi" ("1,000 keys protest"), a symbolic initiative involving the inhabitants of the area, who were protesting against the impossibility of accessing their own houses. Hanging their house keys on the barriers that blocked access to the red zone, hundreds of people took the streets to protest, showing posters with slogans such as "I was not laughing", "Let's take back our town" or "The debris belongs to us". The citizens breached one of the red zone blockades and broke into Piazza Palazzo, the City Hall square they had not been allowed to see for more than 10 months.

The following Sunday, about 6,000 citizens decided to meet again to conduct another day of protest, to press for the beginning of the rebuilding process, to claim to be an active part of the city reconstruction, and to recall media attention to the L'Aquila case. They took with them wheelbarrows, shovels and buckets to remove the debris from the devastated area and to show that, almost a year on – despite all the mainstream media emphasis on the positive aspects of the work of the Italian government – most of the rubble, stones and dirt had not been removed from the centre. Amateur photographers took shots of the event and video-makers also recorded the protest: material was posted and spread on several online platforms (Facebook, Flickr, Photobucket, Picasa, Twitter), and in particular on the most famous online video sharing repository, YouTube. That same afternoon, on Facebook, the popular social network site, a young university student, Federico, founded the group "L'Aquila Wheelbarrows Coordination" ("Coordinamento Carriole Aquilane"). The main aims of the group were:

- to involve citizens in decision processes regarding L'Aquila reconstruction, contrasting with the government's top-down approach;
- to ask for the re-opening of the red zone;
- to sensitise public opinion on the issue of the debris removal and the consequent historical centre reconstruction;
- to promote transparency in the management of the disaster funds.

Those residents-turned-activists were labelled by the mainstream media as "The People of the Wheelbarrows" (hereafter "PoW"). Citizens decided to meet every Sunday to clean the red zone and established a permanent assembly. Participants also met every Wednesday and Sunday evening at 6.00 p.m. in the main square (Piazza Duomo) to discuss ideas, perspectives, and action.

Literature review and research questions

Social movements and ICTs

In the last two decades, a growing literature in social movements and alternative media research has dealt with the relationships between social movements and information and communication technologies (ICTs), focusing in particular on the Internet. ICTs have a variety of effects on the mobilising structures of social movements, opportunity structures, and framing processes (for a review of the literature, see Garrett 2006, Lievrouw 2011, Treré 2012).

On the one hand, the Internet is said greatly to facilitate mobilisation and participation in traditional offline activism, such as national street demonstrations, extending the traditional arsenal of protest movements to include electronic tools (emails, online petitions, etc.) and giving them a more transnational character by diffusing communication and mobilisation efforts rapidly and effectively (Bennett 2003, Cammaerts & Van Audenhove 2005, Della Porta & Mosca 2005). On the other hand, the Internet is seen as creating new forms of activism and resistance (Costanza-Chock 2003, Van Laer & Van Aelst 2009).

The emergence of Web 2.0 technologies like social networking platforms (Google+, Facebook, FriendFeed, etc.), microblogging platforms such as Twitter, blogs and video-sharing sites such as YouTube or Vimeo have provided activists and movements with increased opportunities to spread information, and organise and coordinate online actions (Chadwick 2009, Kavada 2012). The case of the contemporary Italian student movement has shown that arguing that these new technological possibilities are necessarily adopted by activists is a subtle form of technological determinism (Barassi & Treré 2012) that can blind researchers to exploration of the use of other "banal" practices related to "old" technologies (email, forums, etc.), whose relevance can be crucial to movement repertoires.

Moreover, the debate regarding the usefulness of social media within social movements has taken off thanks to the waves of mobilisation that shocked the world in 2011. From the Arab insurrections, to the Spanish Indignados and the Occupy Movement in the USA, to the so-called Chilean Winter and the Movement for Peace with Justice and Dignity in Mexico, 2011 will be remembered as an exceptional year of resistance all over the world or, as *Time* magazine puts it, "the year of the protester".[1]

The effectiveness of social media for social movements is a controversial topic.

On the one hand, some have pointed to the advantages that social media bring to activism, such as the possibility of facilitating the creation of a "shared awareness", that is, "the ability of each member of a group to not only to understand the situation at hand but also to understand that everyone else does, too" (Shirky 2011, pp. 35–36). On the other hand, critics point out that social media are only able to create "weak ties" among activists and underline the risks related to "clicktivism" (Gladwell 2010), warning that these platforms tend to facilitate weak forms of engagement such as clicking "like" on Facebook causes. Moreover, the risks of surveillance and control inherent in Web 2.0 platforms (Farinosi 2011a, 2011b, Morozov 2011)

---

[1]   *Time*, Person of the Year: The Protester, Dec. 26, 2011. http://www.time.com/time/covers/europe/0,16641,20111226,00.html.

apply even more to the case of activists' media practices. Gerbaudo (2012) has rightly pointed out that both techno-optimist and techno-pessimist approaches tend to essentialise social media, and we need instead to explore their appropriations in specific local contexts and geographies.

Regarding the Italian context, the case of comedian Beppe Grillo and the importance of online communication strategies for his political success has been addressed in various studies (among others: Lanfrey 2011, Pepe & Di Gennaro 2009), and the use of online communication by the Italian student movement which emerged in 2008 to fight against the subordination of knowledge to the neoliberal system has also been explored (Treré 2012).

Multiple online technologies and online/offline dimensions in activism

It has been stressed that studies on social movements and the media often fall into the trap of the "one-medium bias", the persistent privileging of the analysis of just one medium or platform (Treré, 2012). The literature has generally failed to recognise issues obvious to activists such as the use by social movement actors of multiple platforms and their engagement in a wide array of online activities. Most studies talk about "the Internet" but do not make any distinction between the constellation of activities regarding multiple technologies, applications and platforms that can be used online. Baym et al. (2004) have warned that compiling online activities into a single variable of Internet use disregards important differences in the nature of the activities performed. Whereas some online activities are social, others are performed at the individual level. Moreover, within social online activities, a wide range of options is available, such as email, chat, IM, wikis, blogs and several social media platforms.

In recent analyses of movements and their media, different authors (among others: Barassi & Treré 2012, Costanza-Chock 2012, McCurdy 2011, Mattoni 2012, Kavada 2012, Padovani 2013, Treré 2012) have successfully shown how to overcome the bias and consider the whole "repertoire of communication" (Mattoni 2012, 2013) with which activists interact. Social movement actors often simultaneously use different types of Internet technologies and platforms to perform different activities for diverse purposes: we thus need to take into account the technological complexity of the Internet for a better grasp of the full range of online activities that social movements carry out.

Therefore, in this paper we ask: how do the PoW interact with the Internet to organise collective action? We pay particular attention to the array of platforms and online technologies used by activists of the PoW and, furthermore, we explore the interplay between the online and offline dimensions in the PoW's practices.

The second aspect we explore in this chapter is the interplay between the online and offline dimensions in the PoW's practices. Most social movement studies do not provide a deep understanding of the online/offline dynamics of social movements or how activists merge online activities with more traditional practices carried out offline. In our view, many social movement studies have relied on too marked a separation between the online and the offline dimensions, replicating dichotomies such as the virtual and the real. This line of thought can be found not only in the first studies on social movements and ICTs but also in more recent works. For instance, McCoughey and Ayers affirm that:

> The Internet allows us to interact with others without our voices, faces and bodies. [...] The Internet thus raises new questions about social change and how it works. For instance, where is the body on which that traditional activism has relied? (2003, p. 5)

In our view, studies should avoid replicating the real-virtual dichotomy (Papacharissi 2005) in the study of activism. Social movement scholar Mario Diani made an important point when he affirmed that "it is disputable whether the warmth and intensity of direct, face-to-face communication may be found in computer-mediated interactions" (2000, p. 6). There is a necessity, however, not only to investigate if the relationships that we build through ICTs are more "real" or more "trustable", but also to look at how these technologies are integrated into movements' activities and how they are embedded within human discourses and imagination (Barassi 2009). Most studies start directly with the online elements, instead of beginning with the movement's actors and investigating if they do or do not make distinctions between these dimensions and thus if these categories are valuable. As Bennett (2005) has noted with respect to the transnational social justice movement:

> The most important theoretical move we can make in trying to understand the movement is to move beyond the distinction between on- and offline relationships. Technology is often aimed at getting people together offline, and one purpose of offline associations is often to clarify and motivate online relations. (Bennett 2005, p. 217)

There is a need for a better understanding of the continuous blending, combination and interplay of online and offline practices within social movements and this understanding should come from analyses whose focus is represented by the actors. Social movements continuously operate by shifting and blending the online and offline dimensions, and it is in this never-ending combination that they organise, mobilise and protest. The erosion of dichotomies is well explained by Gillan (2009) who, in his work on the anti-war movement, advises us to conceptualise the role of the Internet with care. This scholar does not consider that the Internet provides an alternative space for social movements or that it constitutes a tool for movements to create social change.

> Rather, Internet activities are understood as partially constitutive of social movements. That is, as the distinction between "virtual" and "real" has eroded, so the creation and dissemination of meaning through Internet technologies has been included among the core practical tasks of movement organizations (2009, p. 26).

Atton (2004) rightly argued that we need to recognise the banality of Internet practices, meaning not their triviality, but a focus on the ways in which these practices are embedded into activists' everyday activities. The focus of this chapter is thus not on the supposed virtualisation of the movement owing to the adoption of Internet technologies. As suggested by Slater (2002), we do not take the online/offline categories for granted, but start with activists' media uses to see if the PoW make a distinction between the online and the offline, and "if they do, when and why they do it, and how they accomplish it practically" (p. 543).

The vision of the Internet as a "separate sphere", a "distinct world" that pulls people away from their everyday lives and social circle, no longer holds in the light of recent research showing that the Internet integrates with people's everyday practices (Boase & Wellman 2006, Matei & Ball-Rokeach 2002). As Wellman has recently pointed out, "both interpersonal scholars and contentious politics scholars have had to show the intertwining of online and offline activity: they are not separate lives" (2010, p. 151). Castells (2009) observes that the space of the new social movements in the digital age is at the same time constituted by the space of flows and the space of places. Social movements continuously operate through shifting and blending the online and the offline world, and it is precisely through this combination that they organise, mobilise and protest. In the L'Aquila case the interplay and continuity between the online and offline dimensions is particularly strong and represents a unique case in the Italian scenario.

Therefore we ask how the movement's participation is articulated between online spaces and offline squares, meetings and events.

Methodology and theoretical framework

In order to understand how the PoW interact with the Internet to organise, spread and report collective action and how the activists' participation is articulated between online spaces and offline squares, we deployed a multi-method approach, combining different qualitative research tools, in order to provide a more complete set of findings and obtain a deeper understanding of the movement. As highlighted by Klandermans and Staggenborg: "A major advantage of social movement research has been the use of multiple methods... Triangulation of methods ultimately produces stronger theories than multiple replications and permutations of the same method" (2002, pp. 315–316). We therefore conducted 20 semi-structured interviews, online content analysis and non-participant observation, and focused our attention on the exploration of the media practices of the activists of the PoW.

The choice of methods was informed by approaches that look at activists' media as practice (Brauchler & Postill 2010). The analysis of media as practice requires moving beyond functionalist approaches which only understand media as text (Couldry 2004).

Recent works on social movements (Barassi & Treré 2012, McCurdy 2011, Mattoni 2012, Treré, 2012) have developed theoretical and methodological lenses to explore activists' media practices. Although scholars do not agree on a specific definition of media practice, they all concur about using different sets of methodologies to explore the array of technologies which activists use and try to understand what social movement actors "actually do" with these multiple platforms.

In the exploratory phase, we spent a month observing the official Facebook group of the PoW, formally known as "L'Aquila Wheelbarrows Coordination" ("Coordinamento Carriole Aquilane"[2]), and, on the basis of the number of posts, interactions and comments published on the wall, we selected some of the most active members of the online group. We contacted them and carried out semi-structured interviews with a convenient sample of 20 individuals (11 males and 9 females) of different ages (average age: 36.5 years) and backgrounds. Semi-structured interviews are pivotal for understanding social movements from the point of view of participants (Blee & Taylor 2002) because they allow activists the freedom to express their

---

[2]   http://www.facebook.com/?ref=logo#!/group.php?gid=333399523599&ref=ts.

visions in their own terms and can provide reliable and comparable qualitative data. Furthermore they are particularly relevant for the exploration of how activists regard their participation and how they understand and make sense of their social world. Interviews were digitally recorded and then transcribed for thematic analysis (Flick 2009).

In a second phase, we explored the online activities of the members of the movement, investigating the tactics behind the adoption of multiple Internet platforms for the production and/or distribution of content. In particular, we focused our attention on the Facebook group "L'Aquila Wheelbarrows Coordination", which was by far the most used online platform, with 3,318 members. We took into account three months of the online group's activity, from 28 February, when the group was opened, to 31 May 2010, and analysed the kind of content activists shared on the Facebook wall with the other members of the group. We conducted online content analysis (Byrne 2007, Herring 2010), in order to provide a more fine-grained understanding of the messages posted on the wall and categorised the data collected on the basis of their content (text/photo/video).

In addition, we decided to conduct brief offline ethnography by spending five Sundays with the PoW. We took part in their *scarriolate* (a neologism coined by the group's activists, with the idiomatic meaning of "to go down to the square with a wheelbarrow") in the red zone and participated in several town meetings.

The combination of different methods allowed us to get a wide picture of the movement's media practices and to develop a model, the "Integrated System of Local Protest" (ISoLP), that summarises the combination of the three different phases identified from the data analysis.

Findings: An integrated system of local protest

From the interviews we carried out it emerged that the PoW have used a variety of online platforms – blogs, online journals, social network sites – to be informed, to post material (photos, videos, texts) and to spread messages and coordinate themselves. Their practices highlight the tendency of contemporary networked movements to spread over a wide range of online platforms. Furthermore some of the movement's activists also wrote articles for local (*Il Capoluogo*) or national newspapers (*Il Fatto Quotidiano*) and participated in TV programs on the national RAI networks (*Porta a Porta* on RAI 1 and *Anno Zero* on RAI 3). That means that there is not only an adoption of several online platforms but also a variety of crossovers among different media. As highlighted by Padovani (2013), activists in L'Aquila have simultaneously used the four strategies of interactions with mainstream media identified by Rucht (2004): abstention, attack, adaptation, alternative.

People adopted different online platforms for different purposes, depending on the technical architecture and characteristics of each online environment. In this context it is possible to identify three distinct phases:

1. *planning phase*, in which activists organised and promoted events, town meetings and, more generally, all the activities of the movement;

2. *square phase*, offline moments in which activists carried out their initiatives, such as *scarriolate* or town meetings;

3. *report phase*, in which members of the movement used media to report – through textual and/or visual content – what happened during the meetings in the square.

In the planning phase, the most commonly used online tool was the "event" box of the Facebook group "L'Aquila Wheelbarrows Coordination". A small group of administrators used this Facebook feature to create a webpage in order to advertise a particular initiative (such as assemblies, Sunday *scarriolate* or meetings) and to send an invitation with details about a specific event to all the members of the Facebook group. The construction of an event-page on Facebook is quite an easy task, consisting of filling in all the details about the initiative (name, time, date, location and a brief summary of what the event is about) and inviting people to attend it. This allowed the actors of the movement to promote their activities among the Aquilani exiled after the earthquake to hotels on the Adriatic coast or accommodation provided by the Italian Civil Protection in other cities, such as Pescara, Chieti, Teramo, or in other municipalities in the province of L'Aquila away from the epicentre, like Sulmona and Avezzano. Thanks to Facebook they could be informed about the grassroots initiatives taking place in the city and reconnect their ties with the community.

From the analysis of the interviews, Facebook represented the online platform used most often by the members of the PoW and citizens of L'Aquila in the post-earthquake phase. The social media were used differently in the different stages of the post-earthquake phase. In the earliest moments after the tragedy, Facebook was mainly used to communicate from individual profiles to networks of friends and spread information about people who had been rescued, people who were found dead under the rubble, and people who were still missing. The role of Facebook was pivotal in a second phase, when it was used to find friends and reconnect with them, given that the centre and the traditional social spaces had been destroyed by the quake and many inhabitants had been displaced in the tent-camps or in other cities. Furthermore, Facebook was crucial even after the emergency phase, as a space for discussion and aggregation, and it played a key role in helping the construction of the PoW movement. According to Giusi, blogger and activist (female, 52 years old):

> Everything happened online, because all the people who are now in the assemblies had a Facebook profile so we created a "tom-tom".

As another activist explained to us:

> The Web was important because obviously the squares do not exist anymore, there are no physical spaces to meet and the virtual square became Facebook, the blogs and forums where citizens and committees exchange ideas and give appointments (Francesco, journalist and activist; male, 28 years old).

Talking about the PoW movement, Alessio pointed out:

> With Facebook we absolutely created the movement. We exploited the social network to make people conscious of their being political citizens and take responsibility regarding the power system, so the first time there was a break in the historical centre it was thanks to a Facebook group (Alessio, activist of the "3e32" no-profit citizen network; male, 35 years old).

From 28 February, the day on which the group was founded, to 31 May 2010, activists of the PoW promoted 18 Facebook events through the Facebook group "L'Aquila Wheelbarrows Coordination". The strong organisational function of the Facebook group also emerged from the Web content analysis of the messages and comments written by members on the wall. The most common words are: L'Aquila, *piazza* (square), *Domenica* (Sunday), *carriole* (wheelbarrows), *macerie* (debris). The first two words indicate the location of the event, the third refers to the day of the offline meeting, the fourth suggests what citizens should bring with them to take part in the protest and the fifth shows the main object of activists' attention, the debris, which had to be carefully collected and removed from the red zone.

Each event posted on Facebook comes with a flyer (see for example Figures 4.1 and 4.2) produced by an amateur graphic designer active in the movement and both uploaded online and posted up on the walls of the city in order to announce the demonstration and remind people of the tools they need to bring with them for the action (wheelbarrows, gloves, buckets, safety helmets, surgical masks, cameras).

Figure 4.1. Flyer of the 11/04/2010 Sunday *scarriolate*

Source: http://www.facebook.com/photo.php?fbid=1344621370167&set=o.333399
523599&type=1

Figure 4.2. Flyer of the 09/05/2010 Sunday *scarriolate*

Source: http://www.facebook.com/photo.php?fbid=1368649210848&set=o.33339
9523599&type=1

Another important online tool used during the planning phase was the
website "L'Aquila Anno Uno-Spazi Aperti per una Agenda Aquilana"
("L'Aquila Year One-Open Spaces for an Aquilana agenda")[3], an online space
where citizens could obtain information on activities organised by members

---

3   Formerly at http://www.anno1.org/home.

of the PoW, put forward a proposal, share suggestions for the reconstruction of the city, comment on what other people had written and read reports of previous meetings. The proposals received online were then discussed offline during the citizens assembly, thus providing the opportunity for participation in town meetings to citizens who could not take part in the assemblies directly because of distance.

During the square phase all the initiatives promoted by the activists of the PoW through the Facebook group and the site anno1.org were carried out offline. The offline dimension was characterised by two key meetings and subsequent activities which took place intensively from February to June 2010:

- the town meeting: citizens gathered every Wednesday and Sunday evening at 6.00 p.m. in a big tent located in the centre of the main square (Piazza Duomo) of L'Aquila to discuss ideas regarding the reconstruction of the city;

- the Sunday *scarriolate*, a community team, in which each citizen made a contribution: every Sunday morning they met downtown to make a human chain, passing pails from hand to hand to remove the debris and clean up the centre.

The town meetings were based on the S-OST technique, a method based on self-organisation and participants' opportunity to make proposals. It was tested for the first time in Florence (Italy), mixing elements from the OST (Open Space Technology), created by Harrison Owen (2008), and elements from the E-TM (Electronic Town Meeting) system. The activists of the PoW decided to adopt this method and to adapt it to their local context and needs, trying to recreate spaces for open dialogue after the disaster. The S-OST meetings were mainly based on two different levels: discussion panels and plenary assembly. Discussion panels were self-managed by a small group of participants with the help of several expert coordinators and were based on three macro-topics: (1) reconstruction of the urban context; (2) reconstruction of the social fabric; (3) reconstruction of the economic fabric. All the panels were based on the "law of two feet", which, as an activist explained us, consists in the following principle: "if you're in a situation where you are neither learning nor offering your contribution, use your two feet and go somewhere else!". At the end of the panel sessions, the three groups of citizens converged in the plenary assembly where they presented a summary of the major issues emerging from the different panels and discussed the results with all participants in the plenary assembly.

At the end of the plenary meeting, activists of the PoW drafted a report of what happened during the assembly and uploaded the document to the anno1.org website in order to allow those who live at some distance from the city and those who did not attend to know the outcome of the meeting. These reports could in turn be discussed online, in a logic of exchange between the virtual and the real.

The town meetings and the original Sunday *scarriolate* clearly show that in an era characterised by readily accessible digital media, social movements are not virtualised at all, but have learned to use social platforms and integrate them in their practices in order to organise and coordinate their collective actions in the offline dimension, in the squares and in the streets of the city.

The invasion of the red zone with the wheelbarrows represents an act of protest designed to regain possession of the territory and consequently of the narratives concerning the future of citizens. Furthermore it highlights the fundamental importance of the offline dimension. The PoW movement constitutes a significant example of the willingness of citizens to participate in political discourse and of the desire to rebuild together bit-by-bit the social fabric damaged by the tragedy and choose the best options for their future and their city.

As noted, the reports drawn up at the end of town meetings were uploaded to the website anno1.org. During the report phase, however, PoW activists adopted other online platforms. In this phase the Facebook group "L'Aquila Wheelbarrows Coordination" took on a new role and was transformed into a repository for materials created by the citizens during the square phase. Activists used social platforms in order to spread content collected during the offline moments, such as videos or photos, or to comment on what happened during the town meetings. They uploaded to YouTube the videos recorded during the wheelbarrow performance and clips of the most salient features of the assembly. They also used the Flickr platform to post photos of the wheelbarrow demonstration. Sometimes they uploaded videos and photos directly to the Facebook group, but usually they preferred to use YouTube and Flickr and then shared the links on the wall of the Facebook group.

Publishing such content on the Internet gave the opportunity to those who could not attend the event to see and comment on what happened during the meeting and the *scarriolate*, as well as testifying through images to the work done by the PoW activists.

Alongside the social media, other online platforms that played a key role both in the planning phase and in the report phase were blogs. Some of the most active members of the movement in fact have their own personal blogs and posted in-depth articles on what was actually happening in the city, providing their views on issues discussed during the town meetings and on topics related to the post-quake situation. They also recommended guidelines to be followed during the reconstruction process. Usually the message was first posted on the individual blog and then the link was shared both on the individual profile on Facebook and on the Facebook wall of "L'Aquila Wheelbarrows Coordination" in order to increase the visibility of the post. This practice is well illustrated by the words of activist Anna (female, 54 years old):

> I have 5000 contacts on Facebook and I receive something like 70 to 80 friend requests a day… so, you can imagine… When I write a post, usually I write three times per week, because I can't make it otherwise, then the moment I publish the post I immediately put it on Facebook. On Facebook lots of people retake and share it. The classic domino effect.

On the Facebook wall of "L'Aquila Wheelbarrows Coordination" activists posted links to the local or national newspapers in order to share relevant news with the other members of the group, receive comments and spark debate with their fellow citizens. During the three months of activity examined activists shared the following on the wall of the Facebook group "L'Aquila Wheelbarrows Coordination":

- 107 news articles: the vast majority from local newspapers (mainly from *Il Centro* and *Il Capoluogo*), others from some of the major Italian newspapers (*La Repubblica, Il Giornale, Il Corriere*) and a small minority from the international news (*The Times, The Washington Post, Publico*). Usually local newspapers pay more attention than national ones to reporting what is happening in the city and dedicate more space to detailing the news, so it is quite easy for the PoW to find articles that talk about their Sunday *scarriolate* or assemblies;
- 84 posts from personal blogs of the most active members of the PoW movement;
- 71 videos of the town meetings and incursions into the red zone;
- 46 photographs, mainly of the Sunday *scarriolate*.

PoW have also shared the following links (Table 4.1):

Table 4.1. Shared content on the Facebook wall of "L'Aquila Wheelbarrows Coordination" (March to May 2010)

March 2010		April 2010		May 2010	
Links	N.	Links	N.	Links	N.
Articles	72	Articles	24	Articles	11
Blog Posts	49	Blog Posts	23	Blog Posts	12
Videos	37	Videos	16	Videos	18
Photos	37	Photos	4	Photos	5
Total	158	Total	63	Total	41

The report phase marks the culmination of the activities realised by the PoW activists and shows that people adopt different platforms for different purposes, according to their needs and to the technical architecture and the features offered by the applications.

We can summarise the practices described using the following scheme (Figure 4.3):

Figure 4.3. Integrated system of local protest (ISoLP)
Created by M. Farinosi and E. Treré 2013.

As we can see from the description of the activists' practices, the interplay and the overlap between the online and offline activities highlights the existence of an "integrated system of local protest" (ISoLP) that involves multiple online platforms in a never-ending cycle that goes from the Internet to the square and then again to the Internet and characterises the three phases identified in the analysis of our findings. Whereas the first and third phases are closely rooted in the online dimension, the second phase is related to the offline one. The two dimensions are functionally related to each other and their intertwining is especially evident if we take into consideration the role played by social media in the distribution of reports generated from the town meetings. The ISoLP (see Figure 4.3) shows on the one hand how the online and the offline dynamics are both part of a unique continuum, and on the other hand how the different features provided by digital platforms are adopted differently by the PoW activists depending on what they want to achieve.

In the specific case of the PoW, the ISoLP was characterised by the continuous repetition of the cycle of protests that took place during the week (as we have seen, there was usually a *scarriolate* every Sunday morning, and there were town meetings every Wednesday and Sunday afternoon).

Concluding remarks

Our exploration of the media practices of the PoW highlighted the existence of what we have defined as an "Integrated System of Local Protest" (ISoLP) characterised by a complex communication ecology (Treré 2012), based on several crossovers between traditional media and multiple digital technologies and articulated between the online and the offline dimensions: from the strictly online planning phase to the offline square phase (performing the *scarriolate* and taking part in the meetings), and then online again for the report phase.

Digital media have provided new possibilities for mobilisation, organisation, coordination and discussion, offering citizens of L'Aquila new spaces for speaking and acting together, participating in the debate regarding the future of their city. Furthermore, online platforms have allowed the PoW activists to alter mainstream political agendas and use the Internet to post their messages and share their point of view with other citizens.

The PoW's use of social media is part of a process of re-appropriation of public spaces. As we have highlighted in our chapter, activists have adopted different online technologies for different purposes. This reveals the negotiation process between actors and technologies. On the one hand, digital media have affordances (Gibson 1979), and each platform's architecture permits or inhibits certain actions; on the other hand, actors can decide whether to use and how to appropriate through their practices a given platform or a specific part/function of it. Moreover, our work has highlighted that the appropriation of communication technologies by activists has to be analysed in a diachronic perspective, taking into account the different phases of the movement's development. By doing so, we can avoid common generalisations on the role of technology inside movements and provide more nuanced understandings of which particular platform/part of a platform was used during a certain phase and for which purposes. For instance, PoW activists especially used the possibilities provided by Facebook for event creation, and relied on their own website to organise and promote the meetings and the demonstrations. Then, during the report phase, they turned to YouTube, Flickr and blogs, while continuing at the same time to use Facebook and the anno1.org website.

In this case study, the local dimension and the face-to-face relationships have been of considerable importance. Whereas most of the studies on social movements have underlined the role that online platforms play in strengthening the movement's transnational dimension by allowing distant activists to communicate and share resources, our case study shows that digital media can also play an important role in situations that are ingrained in the very local dimension of a specific community. The importance of the locality aspect has been underlined in recent works on social movements and social media (Gerbaudo 2012, Treré 2012). Although social media and Internet platforms in general have played a pivotal role in the development of the actions of the PoW, events, assemblies and informal meetings are still identified by the activists as crucial arenas where the bottom-up participation and the empowerment of citizens find their more complete realisation. In particular, town meetings and Sunday *scarriolate* represented the most emblematic and significant moments of reappropriation of the city and reconstruction of the social fabric, severely compromised by the earthquake of 6 April 2009. In the L'Aquila case, the symbolic importance of the local dimension was strengthened by the fact that the earthquake hit the historical centre, the social and political heart of the city, and wiped out traditional spaces of socialisation. In this context the Sunday *scarriolate* represented a moment of both symbolic and physical reappropriation of citizenship (Farinosi & Treré 2010).

As Padovani (2010) underlines, however, there were also points when the movement built translocal connections in order to gain global attention. Just three months after the earthquake, when the Italian government decided to move the G8 summit to L'Aquila in July 2009 "as a show of solidarity with the town", the two most active protest groups, the "3 e 32 committee" and the Epicentro Solidale (Solidarity Epicentre) movement, used the G8 meeting as a "golden opportunity... to make their voices heard, not only nationally but also internationally", in order to help speed up the rebuilding process. As De Cindio and Schuler have noted (2012), a protest movement focused on a local grievance may also choose to involve a broader audience in order to gain more visibility.

In the literature review, we observed that Morozov underlined the problems related to Web 2.0 technologies as tools of control and surveillance. In our study, this did not represent a concern for PoW activists. When we asked about the risks and threats related to the adoption of social media platforms, interviewees answered that in an emergency situation there was no time to worry about it. Their immediate aim was to reach and connect with as many citizens as possible, so the "dark side" of social media exploitation and control was not considered a relevant issue. Activists chose Facebook because "everyone was there and it was easy to keep in touch and to have a place to meet" (interview with Andrea, activist, male, 32 years old).

Though our contribution has shed light on several aspects of the PoW movement, especially in relation to its media practices, further research is needed to explore other relevant aspects of the PoW case. It has been argued (Treré & Farinosi 2012) that the L'Aquila earthquake was framed by Italian mainstream media as a "spectacle of catastrophe": thus, scholars could profit from deepening the analysis of the connections between the movement and the mainstream media by investigating the differences and the biases in the movement's coverage as provided by local/national television and newspapers. Furthermore, from a more political perspective, it is important to analyse the relationships between the movement and the local/national government in order to see if and how political actors dealt with the proposals and the petitions which emerged from citizens meetings and online discussions.

References

Atton, C. (2004). *An Alternative Internet: Radical Media, Politics and Creativity.* Edinburgh: Edinburgh University Press.

Barassi, V. (2009). Mediating political action: Internet related beliefs and frustrations amongst international solidarity campaigns in Britain. In E. Ardevol & A. Roig (Eds.), *Researching Media through Practices: An Ethnographic Approach. Digithum*, 11, (Online).

Barassi, V., & Treré, E. (2012). Does Web 3.0 come after Web 2.0? Deconstructing theoretical assumptions through practice. *New Media & Society*, *14*(8), 1269–1285.

Baym, N., Zhang, Y., & Lin, M. (2004). Social interactions across media. *New Media & Society*, *6*(3), 299–318.

Bennett, W. (2003). New media power: The Internet and global activism. In N. Couldry & J. Curran (Eds.), *Contesting Media Power: Alternative Media in a Networked World* (pp. 17–37). Lanham, MD: Rowman and Littlefield.

Bennett, W. (2005). Social movements beyond borders: Understanding two eras of transnational activism. In D. Della Porta & S. Tarrow (Eds.), *Transnational Protest and Global Activism* (pp. 203–226). Lanham, MD: Rowman and Littlefield.

Blee, K.M., & Taylor, V. (2002). Semi-structured interviewing in social movement research. In B. Klandermans & S. Staggenborg (Eds.), *Methods of Social Movement Research* (pp. 92–117). Minneapolis, MN: University of Minnesota Press.

Boase, J., & Wellman, B. (2006). Personal relationships: On and off the Internet. In A. Vangelisti & D. Perlman (Eds.), *The Cambridge Handbook of Personal Relationships* (pp. 709–726). Cambridge: Cambridge University Press.

Brauchler, B., & Postill, J. (2010). *Theorising Media and Practice*. New York/Oxford: Berghahn Books.

Byrne, D.N. (2007). Public discourse, community concerns, and civic engagement: Exploring black social networking traditions on BlackPlanet.com. *Journal of Computer-Mediated Communication, 13*(1), 319–340.

Cammaerts, B., & Van Audenhove, L. (2005). Online political debate, unbounded citizenship, and the problematic nature of a transnational public sphere. *Political Communication, 22*(2), 147–162.

Castells, M. (2009). *Communication Power*. USA: Oxford University Press.

Chadwick, A. (2009). Web 2.0: New challenges for the study of e-democracy in an era of informational exuberance. *I/S: Journal of Law and Policy for the Information Society, 5*(1), 1–32.

Costanza-Chock, S. (2003). Mapping the repertoire of electronic contention. In A. Opel & D. Pompper (Eds.), *Representing Resistance: Media, Civil Disobedience and the Global Justice Movement* (pp. 173–191). NJ: Greenwood Press.

Costanza-Chock, S. (2012). Mic check! Media cultures and the Occupy Movement. *Social Movement Studies: Journal of Social, Cultural and Political Protest, 11*(3–4), 375–385.

Couldry, N. (2004). Theorizing media as practice. *Social Semiotics, 14*(2), 115–132.

De Cindio, F., & Schuler, D. (2012). Beyond community networks: From local to global, from participation to deliberation. *Journal of Community Informatics, 8*(3). (Online).

Della Porta, D., & Mosca, L. (2005). Global-net for global movements? A network of networks for a movement of movements. *Journal of Public Policy, 25*(1), 165–190.

Diani, M. (2000). Social movement networks virtual and real. *Information, Communication & Society, 3*(3), 386–401.

Farinosi, M. (2011a). Beyond the panopticon framework: Privacy, control and user generated content. In A. Esposito et al. (Eds.), *Toward Autonomous, Adaptive, and Context-Aware Multimodal Interfaces: Theoretical and Practical Issues* (pp. 180–189). Heidelberg: Springer.

Farinosi, M. (2011b). Deconstructing Bentham's panopticon: The new metaphors of surveillance in the Web 2.0 environments. *Triple C – Cognition, Communication, Co-operation, 9*(1) (Online).

Farinosi, M., & Treré, E. (2010). Inside the "People of the Wheelbarrows": Participation between online and offline dimension in the post-quake social movement. *Journal of Community Informatics, 6*(3). (Online).

Flick, U. (2009). *An Introduction to Qualitative Research*. London: Sage.

Garrett, R. (2006). Protest in an information society: A review of literature on social movements and new ICTs. *Information, Communication & Society, 9*(2), 202–224.

Gerbaudo, P. (2012). *Tweets and the streets: Social Media and Contemporary Activism.* London: Pluto Press.

Gibson, J. (1979). *The Ecological Approach to Visual Perception.* Boston, MA: Houghton Mifflin.

Gillan, K. (2009). The UK anti-war movement online: Uses and limitations of Internet technologies for contemporary activism. *Information, Communication & Society, 12*(1), 25–43.

Gladwell, M. (2010, October 4). Small change: Why the revolution will not be tweeted. *New Yorker.*

Herring, S. (2010). Web content analysis: Expanding the parading. In J. Hunsinger & L. Klastrup (Eds.), *The International Handbook of Internet Research* (pp. 233–250). Berlin: Springer Verlag.

Kavada, A. (2012). Engagement, bonding, and identity across multiple platforms: Avaaz on Facebook, YouTube, and MySpace. *MedieKultur, Journal of Media and Communication Research, 52,* 28–48.

Klandermans, B., & Staggenborg S. (2002). *Methods of Social Movement Research.* Minneapolis, MN: University of Minnesota Press.

Lanfrey, D. (2011). Il movimento dei grillini tra *meetup*, meta-organizzazione e democrazia del monitoraggio. In L. Mosca & C. Vaccari (Eds.), *Nuovi Media, Nuova Politica? Partecipazione e Mobilitazione Online da Moveon al Movimento 5 Stelle* (pp. 143–167). Milano: FrancoAngeli.

Lievrouw, L. (2011). *Alternative and Activist New Media.* Cambridge: Polity Press.

McCaughey, M., & Ayers, M. (2003). *Cyberactivism: Online Activism in Theory and Practice.* New York, NY: Routledge.

McCurdy, P. (2011). Theorizing activists "lay theories of media": A case study of the Dissent! network at the 2005 G8 Summit. *International Journal of Communication, 5,* 619–638.

Matei, S., & Ball-Rokeach, S. (2002). Belonging in geographic, ethnic, and Internet spaces. In B. Wellman & C.A. Haythornthwaite (Eds.), *The Internet in Everyday Life* (pp. 404–427). Hoboken, NJ: Wiley-Blackwell.

Mattoni, A. (2012). *Media Practices and Protest Politics: How Precarious Workers Mobilise.* Farnham: Ashgate.

Mattoni, A. (2013). Repertoires of communication in social movement processes. In B. Cammaerts, P. McCurdy & A. Mattoni (Eds), *Mediation and Protest Movements* (pp.39–57). London: Routledge.

Morozov, E. (2011). *The Net Delusion: The Dark Side of Internet Freedom.* New York, NY: Public Affairs.

Owen, H. (2008). *Open Space Technology: A User's Guide.* San Francisco, CA: Berrett-Koehler Publishers.

Padovani, C. (2010). Citizens' communication and the 2009 G8 Summit in L'Aquila, Italy. *International Journal of Communication, 4,* 416–439.

Padovani, C. (2013). Activists' communication in a post-disaster zone: Cross-media strategies for protest mobilization in L'Aquila, Italy. In B. Cammaerts, A. Mattoni & P. McCurdy (Eds), *Mediation and Protest Movements* (pp.179–205). Bristol UK: Intellect.

Papacharissi, Z. (2005). The real/virtual dichotomy in online Interaction: New media uses and consequences revisited. *Communication Yearbook, 29*(1), 215–237.

Pepe, A., & Di Gennaro, C. (2009). Political protest Italian-style: The blogosphere and mainstream media in the promotion and coverage of Beppe Grillo's V-day. *First Monday, 14*(12). (Online).

Rucht, D. (2004). The quadruple A: Media strategies of protest movements since the 1960s. In W.B. Van De Donk et al. (Eds.), *Cyberprotest. New media, Citizens and Social Movements* (pp. 29–56). New York, NY: Routledge.

Shirky, C. (2011). The political power of social media: Technology, the public sphere, and political change. *Foreign Affairs, 90*(1), 28–41.

Slater, D. (2002). Social relationships and identity online and offline. In L.A. Lievrouw & S. Livingstone (Eds.), *Handbook of New Media: Social Shaping and Consequences of ICTs* (pp. 533–546). London: Sage.

Treré, E. (2012). Social movements as information ecologies: Exploring the coevolution of multiple Internet technologies for activism. *International Journal of Communication, 6,* 2359–2377.

Treré, E., & Farinosi, M. (2012). (H)earthquake TV: "People rebuilding life after the emergency". In A. Abruzzese et al. (Eds.), *The New Television Ecosystem* (pp. 61–79). Berlin: Peter Lang.

Van Laer, J., & Van Aelst, P. (2009). Cyber-protest and civil society: The Internet and action repertoires in social movements. In Y. Jewkes & Y. Majid (Eds.), *Handbook of Internet Crime* (pp. 230–254). Abingdon, UK: Willan.

Wellman, B. (2010). The contentious Internet. *Information, Communication & Society, 13*(2), 151–154.

Chapter 5

EXPANDING THE ACADEMIC RESEARCH COMMUNITY-BUILDING BRIDGES INTO SOCIETY WITH THE INTERNET

ALDO DE MOOR

Academic research is under threat due to factors including lack of resources, fraud, and societal isolation. Such issues weaken the academic research process, from the framing of research questions to the evaluation of impact. After (re)defining this process, we examine how the academic research community could be expanded using the Internet. We examine two existing science-society collaborations that focus on data collection and analysis and then proceed with a scenario that covers expanding research stages like research question framing, dissemination, and impact assessment.

Introduction

Academia is a pillar of the global knowledge society. Academics are traditionally based in universities. Once these were considered ivory towers, safely separate from society. Universities are increasingly pressed, however, to engage much more actively with society, both contributing to the wider life of that society and being more open to its impulses and energies (Jackson 1999, p.105). Instead of the hierarchical organization with isolated, discipline-focused faculties and departments, universities will become much flatter learning organisations, geared towards continuous and collective learning, knowledge sharing, and collaboration (Manlow et al. 2010).

Such an increasing focus on collaboration has been going on within the academy for decades, culminating in virtual "collaboratories", or "laboratories without walls" where scientists are connected to each other, instruments, and data independent of time and location (Finholt 2003). Science we interpret here as all forms of academic research, fundamental or applied. However, new forms of collaborative ties are increasingly being cemented between academics and other stakeholders in society. A case in point here is the growing prominence of the idea of "social innovation", which is essentially about the relationship networks and collaboration processes around new ideas that meet unmet needs (Mulgan 2007). Knowledge institutions such as universities play a key role in these collaborative coalitions, putting their theories and methods to good use, together with other stakeholders like governments, business, and civil society. However, the importance of academia in society goes way beyond such "economic" knowledge considerations. Through its teaching and research, it also helps people to think critically and become knowledgeable and empathetic citizens (Nussbaum 2010). All the more reason to strengthen and expand the ties between the academy and society.

Despite many external pressures, some academic research problems may at least partially arise from the way much of the scientific collaboration process itself is organised. The research process – from asking research questions to measuring impact – is still often organised along traditional intra-academic lines, whereas more outreaching ways are demanded for involving stakeholders, organising workflows, and using digital tools like social media. The purpose of this chapter is to examine the nature of this lack of extra-academic collaboration, to see how that contributes to current academic research problems, and to examine if expanding science-society alliances could make academic research more connected to society.

In this chapter, we first look at some of these core academic research issues (lack of resources, fraud, and societal isolation) from a collaborative perspective in section 2. In sections 3 and 4, we redefine the academic research process and discuss characteristics of a more community-based academic research paradigm. Section 5 outlines a socio-technical research infrastructure that could help expand the academic research community using the Internet. We end the chapter with a discussion and conclusions.

Academic research issues

Scientific research has brought great benefit to humanity and is conducted in a highly professional, distributed academic community. Although most scientific research is of very high quality, there are still issues for im-provement in the academic research process. We outline three examples of general academic research issues, and in the next section will look at how they often manifest themselves in subsequent stages of the research process. Our goal is not to make a comprehensive inventory of these issues, nor to define precisely how they influence the research process. The exact causal mechanisms by which these issues affect the research process are still largely unknown, the issues are co-dependent in many ways, multiple issues affect particular research process stages simultaneously, and so on. Still, by zooming in on how such academic research issues can happen to play out in different research process stages, it becomes easier to identify which (societal) stakeholders are missing and what roles they might play in helping to address these issues.

Lack of resources

Despite its major societal relevance, much of academia is not doing well. External pressures on research universities abound. Rising costs and declining budgets endanger the ability of these institutions to provide quality education, conduct basic science and engineering research that leads to innovations, and perform their public service missions (National Science Board 2012). Such underfunding leads to worrisome practices of young faculty being forced into "volunteerism", instead of being paid a reasonable salary, thus significantly eroding academic research capacity (Kendzior 2012).

Key question: to what extent could extra-academic collaboration help increase research capacity?

Fraud

Science fraud is a much underestimated problem. One meta-study showed that 2% of scientists admitted to themselves having fabricated, falsified or modified data or results; up to one third admitted to other questionable research practices such as dropping data points based on a gut feeling and changing design, methodology or results of a study because of pressure from a funder; rising to up to 72% when asking scientists about the behaviour of others (Fanelli 2009). In the Netherlands, a major fraud case recently occurred. The social psychologist Diederik Stapel turned out to have fabricated most of his research data during his distinguished career, with enormous impact on his direct research colleagues and the field of social psychology as a whole. A thorough committee investigation uncovered many examples of flawed science, including the fabrication, falsification, and unjust replenishment of data, the whole or partial fabrication of analysis results, and misleading presentation of organisation or nature of the experiments. The committee also concluded that the field of social psychology as a whole, by its general uncritical attitude, made the scale and persistence of the intentional fraud – or at least unintentional sloppiness – possible (Levelt Committee et al. 2012). Although this criticism specifically concerns the field of social psychology, it is highly unlikely that all other fields are totally free of such flaws, given that they operate under similar pressures and constraints. By involving other stakeholders with different interests – for example the communities being studied – in co-authoring and evaluating research results, the degree of fraud and sloppiness may be lessened. Of course, these stakeholders may not have the expertise to understand the full implications of sophisticated research methodologies. Still, they, if anyone, should be able to raise the alarm if data purported to be about their communities seem suspicious.

Key question: how are better *checks and balances* built so that fraud cannot grow to such large proportions and stay undetected for such a long time?

Societal isolation

Arguably the most fundamental issue is the "societal isolation" of much of academia. The mass-production university model has resulted in ever-increasing specialisation, leading to a separation between the disciplines where there should be collaboration (Taylor 2009). However, there is also the problem of the scientific community as a whole being too isolated from society. In their early days, universities had to fight for their independence, then from meddling bishops, town governments, kings, emperors and popes (Jones 1999). For many centuries, they were able to do their academic work in splendid isolation. However, since the 20th century, there has been increasing pressure on universities to move back from, for instance in the UK, private, grant-aided institutions doing their own thing to public agencies paid to deliver services wanted by government (Jackson 1999). Although this seems like a step towards the desired more outward focus, unchecked state-controlled science can easily derail into dictates of what should be researched and how to go about this, as Soviet-era research has unfortunately shown. In western science, such extreme state interference is rare. Universities increasingly try to close the gap with society by building voluntary connections with the outside world through grant research projects, research institutes, and communications departments and even science shops. Ever more, universities depend on these connections for broader political support from key local and regional stakeholders (Gurstein 2011). However, despite the promise, current academic research collaborations with the outside world are often constrained to a limited number of (funding) stakeholders, focusing on a narrow research scope, and with projects only lasting a limited period of time. The terms of this involvement are very much set by the academics and universities themselves.

There is a legitimate need for society not only to provide the data (subjects), but also to get more reciprocally involved in framing, executing, and evaluating scientific research. Academics, however, are all too often viewed as part of the "nonproblem", producing unproblematic knowledge that can be distributed to and employed in society. This "outreach model" instead of "engagement" model should be replaced by more reciprocal partnerships of academics with stakeholders representing their own communities (Yapa 2009). This need is obvious in research which directly studies society, as in for example, development research (Chambers 1997). Still, societal involvement in the research process should not be limited to the social sciences. For example, medical research can have a huge potential impact on society as well. An example is the controversy about how research on lethal viruses should be conducted. Such decisions should not be left to the scientists involved alone, but currently, this is too often the case (Enserink 2011).

All this causes many societal issues and interests to be represented insufficiently in academic research. The general problem is that experts intervene in human situations which are complex, uncertain, and unique, while their theories prescribe solutions in terms of simplified causal links. To more fully appreciate such complex real-world situations, these experts need to engage in skilled dialogue with all those stakeholders who (re)present the problems (Jordan 1989, p. 164). This dialogue and mutual learning needs to take place in the form of sustained collaborative partnerships between academic researchers and practitioners (Day & Schuler 2004). For this dialogue, more long-term research communities working on broad research problems and involving a wide range of societal stakeholders are needed.

Key question: how to make academic research communities more *embedded in society*, and have these include societal stakeholders collaborating on broader issues for longer periods of time?

(Re)defining the academic research process

Such major, interacting research process issues make it very hard to see the big picture of what is wrong with much of the current academic research process. Even more difficult is it to come up with concrete and comprehensive "socio-technical designs" of policies, organisational structures, and supporting technologies redressing these problems. To get somewhat of a grip on this complexity, we first give a characterisation of the stages of the academic research process (Table 5.1). For each stage, we mention its often associated stakeholders, typical research process flaws caused by – among other things – the lack of resources, fraud, and societal isolation issues noted earlier, and some directions for collaborative solutions. We use these research process stages as the linking pin between academia and society in the next section. Note that the actors, problems, and solutions mentioned are only selected examples, they are by no means a comprehensive treatment of all actors, problems, and solutions involved in all forms of academic research. Still, these examples should give the reader a flavour of the complexity of both the problem and solution space.

Table 5.1. (Re)defining the academic research process

Research stage	Actors	Problems	Solutions
Research question framing	Academics, funders	Limited scope	Collaborative research partnerships
Data collection and analysis	Academics, few stakeholders (only as patients)	Fraud; sloppy science; lab ≠ world	Citizen researchers
Authoring	Academics	Content, form and participation	Digital storytelling; group report authoring
Review	Academics (peers)	Peer review system outdated, overloaded, biased; promotes conformity	More collaborative process; post-publication review; external stakeholder participation
Dissemination	Publishers, libraries, university departments, academics	Restricted access; no associated data and stakeholder voices	Open access; open data; community/ social media
Impact assessment	---	Non-existent assessment	Social media; long-term collaborative partnerships

Research question framing

Research questions are often framed by academics or by the funders of their studies. Issues that do not meet existing disciplinary or funding priorities typically fall by the wayside. Such narrowly defined research questions do not generally examine the broader social, economic, political, historical or cultural context of the community being studied (Gurstein 2011). One very current and important example concerns the lack of research attention given in the past few decades to the political concept of "the commons". Some say that through narrow neoliberal framing, attention has been focused on promoting the profitability of transnational financial institutions instead of on promoting general welfare through reinvigorating the societal commons (MacLellan & Talpalaru 2012). Had economic and financial academic research been more grounded in reality, and less constrained because of conflicts of interest, these larger societal interests might have been taken into account long before the arrival of the global financial crisis (Scott 2010). Through collaborative research partnerships, such as are being established in well-designed researcher-practitioner communities and social innovation consortia (Day & Schuler 2004, Mulgan 2007), more balanced research question framing can take place. One practical way to improve the societal impact of research is by having students draw on the research skills that they are learning to address community-generated research questions (Strand et al. in Stoecker 2008).

Data collection and analysis

As mentioned in the previous section, data collection and analysis are prone to many forms of fraud and sloppy science (Fanelli 2009, Levelt Committee et al. 2012). Furthermore, academia often has an overly strong focus on rigour instead of relevance. This is not to say that rigour is not important, but that it has colonised relevance, disrupting the balance (Applegate 1999). Lack of relevance is also increased by using artificial, ungrounded lab situations, using, for instance, students as the sole test subjects, and involving none or only few of the many stakeholders actually impacted by the research results. Furthermore, by seeing stakeholders as mere data subjects, instead of active participant researchers, data collection and analysis often leads to less than relevant results (Day & Schuler 2004). Increasingly, however, "citizen researchers" take active role in both data collection and analysis, as we shall see in section 5. To ensure the necessary rigour, academics should properly calibrate their research designs, of course, so that the role and value of the citizen contributions is carefully circumscribed.

Authoring

Authoring is often restricted to academics writing articles for the academic record, such as journals, conference proceedings, and book chapters.

Authoring, however, is much more than simply writing down ideas and findings in formalised text. Three main problems from a stakeholder-perspective concern content, form, and participation. Content and form are restricted to what is permissible in the particular disciplinary genre. Such genres function as sites of interaction enabling access to, structuring and framing participants' actions within groups or organisational contexts, leading to a complex interplay between the texts and the social contexts in which they are produced (Bawarshi & Reiff 2010). Academic texts are typically in the form of highly stylised research papers. However, this excludes non-academic authorial voices such as those of citizens and other societal stakeholders. Unconventional approaches (from an academic genre point of view) such as digital storytelling and stakeholder group report authoring may help amplify such lesser-heard voices in the stakeholder community (Copeland & Miskelly 2010, De Moor 2010). Through new types of content and form, and involving more stakeholders in the re-presentation of reality, academic authoring genres can be enriched to reduce societal isolation and increase research capacity.

Review

Peer review is the core mechanism for separating the academic chaff from the wheat. In traditional blind peer review, submissions are sent to reviewers whose evaluations determine whether papers are accepted, while only the editor communicates with the authors. However, ever more pressing questions are being asked about the effectiveness of peer review. Academics are under increasing pressure to produce visible output, and reviewing is a time-consuming, but unacknowledged activity. It is also far from infallible: Stapel managed to author (at least) 55 fraudulent publications without any of the reviewers noticing (Levelt Committee et al. 2012, p. 25). The current system rewards conformity and allows for considerable bias. Spurred on by technological developments such as the Internet, alternatives are being proposed such as reviews after publication and open, collaborative processes for selecting articles and jointly improving them (Jaschik 2012). Such developments would also open up more the review process to stakeholders from outside academia to identify factual errors and assess analytical interpretations and implications made by the academic authors.

Dissemination

Until recently, academic dissemination was confined to the publication of journals, books, and conference proceedings within the academic community, the publication channels being dominated by the scientific publishers and libraries. University departments such as communication departments; science shops; and "academic fora" were the main outlets for disseminating summaries of these results to the outside world. However, the widespread adoption of the Internet has dramatically increased the options for dissemination of research results. Although the jury is still out on the best business models, open access publishing – where scientific publications will be available for free to anybody interested – will soon be the norm. For instance, the British government has mandated that all publicly funded scientific research must be open access by 2014 (Sample 2012). Still, academic research dissemination will change beyond just wider access to publications. Amongst other purposes, datasets used in the publications will also be made available to double check for fraud and misinterpretation (Levelt Committee et al. 2012). Societal links will be further woven into the academic research publishing process when community media, such as digital storytelling resources,[1] become linked to the open access publications. Such community media could tell the "real world stories" behind academic concepts. At the same time, they provide academics with valuable contacts and case material for future research. Later in this chapter, we will sketch a possible scenario in which this could be made to work.

Impact assessment

Impact assessment, which we define as the long-term evaluation of the validity of academic research after its recommendations have been implemented in the real world, is usually left out of the academic research workflow. It is far too removed from research time-frames and interests for most academics and their institutions to be bothered with. However, impact assessment is essential if the relevance of academic research is to be increased. With the increasing focus on social innovation, power and availability of social media, and more participatory and long-term involvement of external stakeholders in academic research projects, such assessment should become more prominent (Day & Schuler 2004, De Moor 2010). Again, digital storytelling could play an important role here since stakeholder conversations can be recorded and instantly revived years into the future.

---

[1]   See for instance the empowering PhotoVoice "participatory photography for social change" initiative: http://www.photovoice.org/.

Community-based academic research

"The academic/scientific community" is perhaps the largest, best organised, and most thriving professional community in the world. Although consisting of many sub-communities (disciplinary, university, journal, conference, research interest-based, etc.), there is an overarching sense of academic community. This is demonstrated by academia's truly global nature, its shared identity and social norms, its web of intense, interlocking conversations, and so on. Yet, communities which alongside "bonding" social capital (strong ties within groups) also have "bridging" social capital (weak ties across groups) are the most effective in organising for collective action (Kavanaugh et al. 2005). This bridging role of academia is still underdeveloped, as there remain many external societal communities that academic research should build enduring collaborative bridges into (Day & Schuler 2004). When such inter-group bridging collaboration is supported by the Internet, both bonding and bridging capital is further increased, as the Internet helps maintain social relations, exchange information, and increase face-to-face interaction (Kavanaugh et al. 2005).

What is the role of these community-based partnerships mediating between science and society? Characteristically, they connect stakeholders from both the academic and societal spheres in new and meaningful ways, resulting in deep levels of collaboration (Leavy 2011, p. 88). This is not to say traditional disciplinary academic research is without merit. It is still a foundation of science, and, especially in the natural sciences, the primary mode of operation. However, according to Leavy, disciplinary research is increasingly contextualised in transdisciplinary research, when the research problem, issue, or question instead of the "home" discipline is at the centre of the research process. This transdisciplinarity is not a method, but an approach involving the integration of multiple disciplines in a project aimed at a social, human, or "life-world" purpose. It leads to the development of new conceptual, theoretical, and methodological frameworks (Leavy 2011, pp. 24–33, 52).

How does this expanded academic research process work? First, it is gradually moving in four steps from "research on communities" to "research by communities". In "research on communities", communities are seen as passive objects. "Research for communities" is done by outsiders, but presented as under the control or in the interest of the local community. In "research with communities", communities are engaged as partners with the (academic) researcher. Finally, the most empowering form of research

– "research by communities" is where the community undertakes main elements of the research, with the academic researcher only providing support (Gurstein 2011). Of course, the exact level of engagement required depends on the situation, but the trend is one towards more control and peer status of the non-academic co-researcher. A case in point is the example where a partnership with community organisations and residents helped academics rethink their theory on poverty in totally different ways (Yapa 2009).

In the remainder of this chapter, we investigate how the academic research community could be expanded through more structured Internet-mediated research process collaboration between science and society (Figure 5.1). What we are looking for are new and meaningful ways of establishing sustainable collaborative alliances between members from the "core" academic research community (such as academics, publishers, science funders, and various university institutional actors) and external stakeholders (including citizens, governments, business, NGOs etc.). The Internet, being a communications "network of networks", is to play a core enabling role in these collaborations.

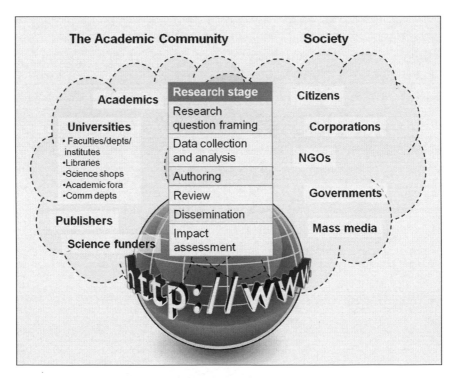

Figure 5.1. Expanding the academic research community

Expanding the academic research community with the Internet

A new paradigm is emerging in which the university is no longer a traditional one-way research and teaching organisation, but a network of communities working on collective learning, knowledge sharing and collaboration. Social media can help in implementing these principles through supporting "the five Cs": communication, collaboration, community, creativity, and convergence (Manlow et al. 2010). It is often assumed that with the rise of social media, collaboration will self-organise. Nothing is less true. Collaboration, especially when ICT-mediated, requires careful socio-technical design to get from users merely reading and liking individual posts to becoming involved in complex, long-term, multi-stakeholder collaboration processes (Preece & Shneiderman 2009).

In this section we show two such existing socio-technical collaborations: Galaxy Zoo which includes citizens as participant researchers in data analysis, and PatientsLikeMe, doing the same for data collection and analysis. We then include a not-so-hypothetical scenario for how a mix of existing organisational university infrastructure and social media could help build similar sustainable alliances for other research workflow stages like research question framing, dissemination, and impact assessment.

Expanding data analysis: Galaxy Zoo

Galaxy Zoo[2] is part of The Zooniverse. This is a collection of web-based Citizen Science projects that use the efforts and abilities of volunteers to help researchers deal with the flood of data that confronts them. Participants are asked to classify galaxies according to their shapes (Figure 5.2). The initial project resulted in the classification of nearly 900,000 galaxies. Started in 2007, 70,000 classifications an hour were done within 24 hours of launch. This has resulted in over 50 million classifications in the first year, contributed by over 150,000 people.[3]

Interestingly, each galaxy is classified by many different, randomly assigned participants. This should help to considerably increase the reliability of data analysis, and to reduce errors and fraud, as compared to traditional ways of interpreting data by academics without citizen support. One mechanism by which this may happen is simply the sheer number of citizen researchers. Whereas in "academic-only" research many data points are only interpreted

[2]   http://www.galaxyzoo.org.
[3]   http://www.galaxyzoo.org/#/story (accessed 9 June 2013).

by one or two analysts, in massively-scaled research, such as Galaxy Zoo, numerous interpreters of the same data may be available, making it much harder to massage away undesirable data, for example. However, although citizens play such an important role in classification, they likely have a much smaller role to play in the subsequent interpretation of these data, given the theoretical complexity of astronomical research.

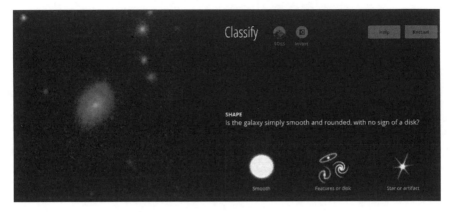

Figure 5.2. Classifying galaxies with Galaxy Zoo[4]

Expanding data collection and analysis: PatientsLikeMe

PatientsLikeMe[5] (Figure 5.3) is a global data-driven social networking health site. It allows its members to share information about symptoms and treatments, initially only for rare and life-changing conditions, but as of early 2013 having over 200,000 patients on its platform and covering 1,800 diseases (Upbin 2013). Patients can compare their conditions to those with similar afflictions. Members can participate free of charge in clinical trials. A commercial service exists for pharmaceutical companies to get in touch with patients of interest. Several collaboration partnerships have been set up with research and academic institutions. PatientsLikeMe calls itself "a for-profit company with a not just for profit attitude", carefully aiming to align individual, academic, and business interests.

From an academic research point of view, citizens act as data collecting and somewhat analysing researchers (from their personal perspective), as do research companies on the organisational level. Compared to Galaxy Zoo, it is interesting to see how commercial stakeholders have been woven into

---

4   Source: http://www.galaxyzoo.org/#/classify (image captured 9 June 2013). Reproduced with permission of Galaxy Zoo.

5   http://www.patientslikeme.com.

the collaboration. Given the complexity of the data collection and analysis activities and the sensitivity of ethical issues like privacy, the collaborative network is quite a bit more complex than in the Galaxy Zoo case.

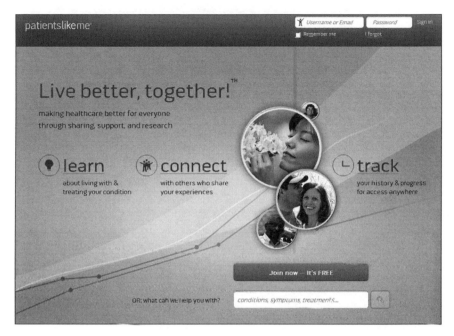

Figure 5.3. Collecting and analysing patient data with PatientsLikeMe[6]

Expanding research question framing, dissemination and impact assessment

Most science-society collaborations revolve around data collection and analysis, as in the cases of Galaxy Zoo and PatientsLikeMe. However, some stages of the research process depicted in Figure 5.1 are not yet covered, and if so only with few of many possible stakeholders involved, and then often only with low degrees of participation. Is there a way to expand the academic research in a scalable and sustainable way in these other stages as well? To sketch the opportunities for building new bridges, we briefly examine a hypothetical, but plausible scenario.

In the scenario, we focus on the question of whether we could create more and lasting connections between academia and external stakeholders through social (people) and technical (tool) "linking pins". A precondition

---

6   Source: http://PatientsLikeMe.com (image captured 9 June 2013). Reproduced with permission of PatientsLikeMe.

for the scenario to be plausible is that it should be more about connecting existing webs of conversations than creating new ones (De Moor 2012). This is essential since resources are scarce, and it is neither possible nor desirable to start all kinds of separate research conversations from scratch. We next look at some social linking pins (the "science communicating" organisational units in the university) and two technical linking pins (social videos and social bookmarking sites).

Social linking pins: The university science-society communicators

Most individuals and organisational units in universities are in the business of communicating. Academics constantly communicate with stakeholders within and beyond the university, which is the essence of research as a collaborative process. Their organisational units (faculties and departments) also communicate with the outside world, but their core process is often intra-university communications, in order to structure and support the primary research and education process. However, there are units in most universities that specialise in science-society communications. Key examples are communications departments, academic fora/Studium Generale, and science shops. Science shops were established, for instance, in the Netherlands in the 1970s to build working relationships between universities and citizen groups that need answers to relevant questions (Leydesdorff & Ward 2005). Likewise, Studium Generale[7] is a faculty-independent department at all Dutch universities that organises lectures, discussions, courses, and programs around science, art and culture. The activities are primarily aimed at university students and staff, but also accessible to outsiders. These organisational units are natural social linking pins with society.[8]

Technical linking pins: Video servers and social bookmarking sites

The Internet in general and social media in particular are especially powerful technologies to help connect, scale, and amplify conversations into meaningful webs (De Moor & Aakhus 2013). Given our focus on feasibility, the supporting tools should act as "bridging technologies", connecting

---

[7]   http://www.studiumgenerale.nl/. At Tilburg University, Studium Generale is called Academic Forum, which clearly indicates its bridging role.

[8]   There are many more science-society communicators in universities. For instance, Tilburg University participates in TiSIL, a joint initiative of four regional higher education institutes in the region that aims to facilitate social innovation through the creation, dissemination, and application of interdisciplinary knowledge. Another such communicator is the Science Hub Brabant, which aims to interest primary school children in the province in scientific research.

conversations rather than requiring many extra resources in order for collaborators to produce all content from scratch. The tools used should be widely available, not take too much effort to use, and connect existing online and offline conversations. We distinguish two such bridging technologies in this scenario: social videos (e.g. YouTube) and social bookmarking technologies (e.g. Diigo).

Digital storytelling

Digital storytelling is useful in boundary-crossing settings. Digital stories can help strengthen the sense of community, serve as boundary objects mediating relationships, and elicit stories from overlapping communities (Copeland & Miskelly 2010). YouTube[9] is a videosharing website on which users can upload, view, share, and comment upon videos. It is available everywhere, very easy to use and free. As such, it meets the bridging technologies criteria.

Social bookmarking

Research publications are classified, often by libraries, using formal taxonomies and ontologies. However, increasingly popular on the Web are "folksologies" in the form of social bookmarking sites. Such folksologies provide informal semantics and can be created and adopted by anybody on the Internet (Spyns et al. 2006). Since different stakeholders can label the same resources (e.g. publications, video stories) with their own terminology, social bookmarking sites are a bridging technology par excellence. Diigo[10] is one of the most popular social bookmarking sites, allowing individuals, and also communities and organisations, to upload, access and share bookmarks with each other and the world.

Scenario: Connecting research question framing, dissemination and impact assessment

We outline a hypothetical but not too far-fetched scenario of a feasible "communications architecture" that uses both the social and the technical linking pins mentioned above. It is set at Tilburg University, as this university has already an intensive collaboration between its different science-society communicators. In the scenario, we investigate what an expanded and more integrated collaborative research question framing, dissemination, and impact assessment process could look like.

---

[9]   http://www.youtube.com.

[10]   http://www.diigo.com.

Research question framing

2013. At Tilburg University, Academic Forum organises a series of debates on the financial crisis. It will soon hold a debate on the key question: "What Caused the Financial Crisis and How to Prevent the Next One?" It invites several of its own university academics, as well as a politician, a banker, and somebody working for a concerned citizens-group.

The Science Shop, in the meantime, has several students doing final-year research projects on the crisis, supervised by the stakeholders invited for the debate. One student is doing a literature review for the academics involved. A university librarian has extracted a taxonomy of the most relevant scientific terms related to the topic of the crisis. Using the terms from this taxonomy, the student finds several publications related to the topic in the library database. The Academic Forum discussion leader uses these publications in the preparation of the debate.

The other students – supervised by the external stakeholders – work on their own reports. As part of their case research, they use digital storytelling techniques to interview stakeholders on how the crisis impacts them and how they think it should be solved. They upload the videos to YouTube. As part of their research chores, they also index video fragments on Diigo. To this purpose, they tag each fragment with the "official" taxonomy tags. However, they also add the informal terms used by the stakeholders to further index the fragments. They compare each other's mark-up on video fragments covering similar research concepts. Interestingly, they find that they have all used similar scientific taxonomy tags for fragments covering similar topics, but the informal terms used vary widely, as the banker, for instance, was using much more jargon than the citizen interviewed.

In preparing the debate, the Academic Forum discussion leader monitors what's hot in the mass media. Using the "ordinary language" terminology prevailing in newspapers and on TV, she searches Diigo on these terms. She finds two video interview fragments uploaded by the students that would really bring the message home to the audience, and selects them as introductory fragments for the debate.

As the debate takes place, it is videotaped. Afterwards, the Academic Forum research assistant uploads the video on YouTube and marks up the debate fragments on Diigo, using the same scientific taxonomy and informal folksonomy as used/produced by the Science Shop students. In particular, he distils some fragments that cover the key research questions which the participants agreed upon are still wide open.

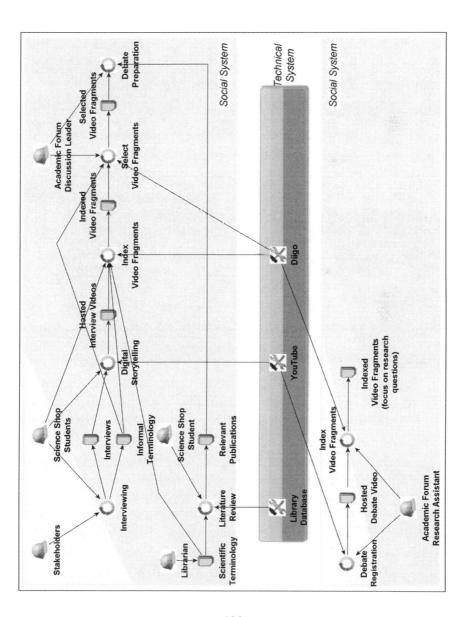

Figure 5.4. A partial communications architecture of the "research question framing" stage

Figure 5.4 presents a (partial) communications architecture of the research question framing stage. Similar architecture diagrams could be drawn for the other stages. Clearly distinguished are the various roles (Stakeholders, Science Shop Students...), key workflows (Interviewing, Digital Storytelling...), results (Interviews, Informal Terminology...) and tools used (Library Database, YouTube, and Diigo).

Several observations can be made. First of all, the architecture looks complex. This is because collaborative communication IS complex. Even though systematic design of academic research communication is essential for it to become of higher quality and have more impact, (extra-)academic communication flows are still mostly ad hoc. Whereas the business world invests heavily in solid communications systems and process architectures, the academic research community lags behind.

Second, most of the complexity in the architecture is not in the technical system (their inner workings can be considered black boxes from an architectural point of view), but in their usage context: the social system. Especially in academia, this social system is highly developed, as can be seen from this example. This social complexity should be reflected in its communication systems designs, but is often ignored. Putting it another way, careful socio-technical systems design for collaborative academic research communities generally does not necessarily involve large implementation budgets (all tools mentioned in this scenario are freely available tools in the Cloud). It is, however, about investing in collaboratively – with the community – making sense of how to use and configure these tools in the actual communication context, while translating and embedding these concepts in their daily work processes, and generating a sense of ownership in the users.

Third, even though there is much complexity from an architectural point of view, this does not mean that the individual actors involved need to be aware of this overall complexity. Stakeholders play clearly defined roles and only need to be aware of their own, limited, usage context. For example, the Academic Forum discussion leader can select video fragments simply by searching in Diigo, while the production of these videos and indexing their fragments has already been done separately by Science Shop students. Still, somebody needs to be made responsible for the design of this overall communications architecture. Typically, this responsibility would be assigned to management or the ICT department, in close collaboration with user representatives. End-users would not need to be exposed to these high-level architectural designs, as these can be translated into specific user manuals, task lists, or instruction videos, using their own informal terminologies. Finally, such complex designs would not have to be created from scratch, but could be shared and reused widely as open source reference models by the global academic community, since many of the general communications issues are the same.

Dissemination

Using Diigo, the Tilburg University communications department finds some indexed video fragments that are relevant to their PR purposes, and which they embed on the university website. Several lecturers also search the Diigo site using a mix of professional and informal search terms. A lecturer at the Department of Finance selects several video fragments to illustrate the consequences of risky investment strategies, while a colleague at the Department of Social Psychology uses some fragments (one of them the same) to illustrate the power of group dynamics in corporate decision making and leadership processes. As some students watch these video fragments in preparation for the lectures, they add comments to the videos on YouTube, enriching their meaning for future viewers.

Over time, the growing research video and social bookmarking resources on YouTube and Diigo are also discovered by many external stakeholders. Journalists find them a useful way to quickly identify video material (and possible interviewees for TV shows and newspaper articles), NGOs use them to build activist campaigns around particular issues, companies use selected videos in-house in their Corporate Social Responsibility programs, while school kids use the fragments in their digital homework assignments. In the meantime, through social media like Twitter, Facebook, and blogs, tangential conversations take off, as many stakeholders use the fragments to argue pro or contra the points of view within and across their own communities.

Impact assessment

2023. After the financial crisis was finally kind of overcome in 2018, irresponsible investment behaviours returned with a vengeance. As the global economy had not been reformed in a fundamental way, another crisis hit, even harder than the 2008 one. Academic Forum decides to organise another debate about "What Caused the Financial Crisis and How to Prevent the Next One?" inviting the head of the National Financial Audit department, who used to be an academic himself. The Research That Matters video server is accessed by a reporter preparing a major article for one of the main (digital) national newspapers. It is by now a well-established societal resource, being used for many different purposes by a wide variety of organisations and individuals. While Academic Forum is still in the process of preparing the debate, the reporter finds an interesting 2013 video fragment in which the auditor-then-banker had a completely opposite point of view on what should be done to combat the crisis. She prepares some thorny questions for her planned interview with the auditor who manages to answer most questions satisfactorily. However, a few questions remain unanswered, which form a perfect starting point for the next Academic Forum debate, first replaying those relevant pieces of video from way back…

Discussion

There is no ONE way of doing academic research. There are numerous different paradigms, disciplines, methodologies, traditions, and geographical/cultural factors determining how specific academic sub-communities operate. The examples in this chapter of academic research issues, process stages, and socio-technical solution designs, were necessarily anecdotal. They do not apply in the same way, or at all, to each of the myriad forms in which academic research is organised and conducted. Still, the gist of the argument is that all research has certain problematic issues, that all research is done in stages that need to be adequately defined and calibrated, and that all research needs a well-designed socio-technical collaboration infrastructure. Instead of prescribing a single comprehensive, one-size-fits-all approach, this chapter was merely meant to sensitise the reader to the kind of issues involved, and how to possibly address them, applying a possibly similar but certainly not the exact same analytical approach to their own field.

We have outlined a conceptual framework for analysing science-society collaborations grounded in sustainable stakeholder relations, their interactions being catalysed by the Internet. Such collaborations can help the development of reciprocal relationships between universities and external stakeholders that are respectful, productive and mutually advantageous (Gurstein 2011). These new ways of working together also provide excellent examples of open and social innovation. Open innovation comprises complex, interconnected webs of interacting individuals and organisations focused on producing knowledge-intensive innovative outputs (West & Lakhani 2008). By clarifying and connecting the webs of conversations between these stakeholders, viable new collaborations can be established (De Moor & Aakhus 2013). The related field of social innovation is about "new ideas meeting unmet needs"; how these innovations progress from idea generation through prototyping and piloting, to scaling up and learning; and how effective alliances can be created that cut across organisational, sectoral or disciplinary boundaries (Mulgan 2007). Universities developing the kind of collaborations introduced in this chapter could (and should) be at the forefront of these innovation domains. To do so, from the stakeholders involved, key "collaboration patterns" can be elicited that capture reusable socio-technical lessons learnt. Such patterns represent good and best practices about what research processes done by whom and supported by which tools in what way. They could also be of great help in precisely defining necessary and acceptable checks and balances in the intricate webs of collaborative relationships, workflows, and supporting technical systems (De Moor 2012).

Another field of inquiry to tap into when developing these multi-stakeholder collaborations is community-based research theory and practice. Community-based research serves community-identified needs, is sensitive to the cultural understandings of the community, and supports action around some community-identified issue (Strand et al. in Stoecker 2008). There is a rich community-based research literature and working experience in such overlapping fields as Community-Based Participatory Research and Community Informatics (e.g. Williamson & DeSouza 2007, DCRT 2011, Denison & Stillman 2012). Community-based research concepts, methodologies, ethical principles, and facilitation processes will be very useful in expanding the community-based academic research process. Many institutional barriers need to be overcome to shift the balance of power to the community in community-academy partnerships (Stoecker 2008). Socio-technical communications architectures such as the scenario proposed in this chapter should contribute to lowering these barriers, provided that the architectures are grounded in these community-based research concepts and validated by the community.

How to produce such legitimate communications architectures is still an open question, and could be an interesting extension of community-based research. One particularly promising starting point could be service-learning, by students, that focuses on serving the ICT needs of community organisations. According to Loving et al. (2011), these ICTs can be analysed according to a ladder (or "step stool") of control. At the lowest rung the end-users can put a technology into practice; at the middle rung the end-users can also shape it; and at the top of the ladder the users can even build the tools themselves. Loving et al. (2011) then observe several problems with student service-learning projects, including insufficient assessment of the organisation's ICT goals, rushing to tool selection and implementation, limited student technical development expertise, and the community organisations having unrealistic technical expectations. When students limit their service development to building organisational social media capacity, the projects tend to be more successful, but the authors wonder whether this is enough. From what has been argued in this chapter, we think there is a promising way forward, however. A fourth rung should be added to the ladder: designing the overall socio-technical communication and collaboration system architecture of the community. Much more than in technical wizardry, students' expertise is – or should be – in matching the highly complex and subtle information and communication needs of communities with a wide array of virtual and physical ICTs. Instead of acting as a software engineer, the key role of the students would then be much more that of *systems architect*. Eliciting, interpreting, and translating collaboration patterns that capture socio-technical community needs and constraints should be their core business. By collecting these patterns in bodies of work like pattern languages, such as the Liberating Voices Pattern Language (Schuler 2008), reusable best practices should emerge. By co-creating, configuring, and translating these patterns together with the community, more sense-making, ownership of and empowerment by the ICTs could be realised in the community. Furthermore, such patterns could also be useful in formulating research hypotheses for more traditional academic research outcomes, such as papers and controlled experiments, as they provide tentative relations between independent and dependent variables. These hypotheses could then be tested in various forms of follow-up empirical research.

Opening up the academic research community is essential. More aligned ways of academics working together with societal stakeholders will help deal with such priorities as increasing research capacity, combatting fraud, and lessening the societal isolation of much academic research. However, many of current institutional reforms still look inward. For example, following the Stapel fraud case, the investigation committees made many strong recommendations, including having an independent confidential counsellor for integrity, every PhD student being supervised by at least two (co) supervisors, doing more replications of studies, etc. (Levelt Committee et al. 2012). No expanded science-society academic research collaborations were explicitly proposed, however. In the future, with universities increasingly grounded in and networked with society, more attention will undoubtedly be paid to developing more complete and sound criteria for balanced science-society collaboration systems.

Universities rightly pay much attention to improving their primary processes of research and education. However, there is growing pressure to establish sustainable collaborative partnerships with external stakeholders. As suggested, university science-society communicators like science shops, academic fora, social innovation labs, and communications departments will play increasingly important roles as "brokers" of enduring collaborative relationships. These organisational units are sensitive to both academic and societal needs and preferences, and as such should act as an indispensable bridge. Also, it is important to realise that using the Internet alone is not enough: the many face-to-face events and meetings these science brokers organise bring many diverse stakeholders together. Such physical happenings remain essential for stimulating conversation, building social capital, and trust. Aligning physical and virtual communications is therefore a prerequisite for successful collaboration (De Moor 2012).

Concluding remarks

We live in a transitional time between an often hierarchical, inward-looking, mono-disciplinary-based way of doing science, and the rapidly approaching era of more collaborative, outward-looking and society-focused grounding of academia. By zooming in on the appropriate research issues and process stages, communication architectures for more effective collaborations between stakeholders within and outside of academia can be designed. Each of these socio-technical designs is a strand in the tapestry of strengthened relationships between science and society. Of course, implementing these designs is no panacea, but one by one they will contribute to academic research that is more embedded, sustainable, and relevant.

References

Applegate, L.M. (1999). Rigor and relevance in MIS research: Introduction. *MISQ*, *23*(1), 1–2.

Bawarshi, A.S., & Reiff, M.J. (2010). Genre research in academic contexts. In A. S. Bawarshi & M.J. Reiff (Eds.), *Genre: An Introduction to History, Theory, Research, and Pedagogy* (pp. 107–131). Anderson, SC: Parlor Press.

Chambers, R. (1997). *Whose Reality Counts? Putting the First Last*. London: Intermediate Technology Publications.

Copeland, S., & Miskelly, C. (2010). Making time for storytelling: The challenges of community building and activism in a rural locale. *International Journal of Media, Technology and Lifelong Learning*, 6(2), 192–207.

Day, P., & Schuler, D. (2004). Integrating practice, policy and research. In P. Day & D. Schuler (Eds.), *Community Practice in the Network Society: Local Action, Global Interactions* (pp. 3–20). NY: Routledge.

Durham Community Research Team (DCRT) (2011). Community-based participatory research: Ethical challenges. Centre for Social Justice and Community Action, Durham University.

de Moor, A. (2010). Reconstructing civil society with intermedia communities. *AI & Society*, 25(3), 279–289.

de Moor, A. (2012). Creativity meets rationale: Collaboration patterns for social innovation. In J. Carroll (Ed.), *Creativity and Rationale: Enhancing Human Experience by Design* (pp. 377–404). Berlin: Springer.

de Moor, A., & Aakhus, M. (2013). "It's the conversation, stupid!" – Social media systems design for open innovation communities. In J. E. Lundström, M. Wiberg, S. Hrastinski, M. Edenius & P. J. Ågerfalk (Eds.), *Managing Open Innovation Technologies* (pp. 17–33). Berlin: Springer.

Denison, T., & Stillman, L. (2012). Academic and ethical challenges in participatory models of community research. Information. *Communication and Society*, 15(7), 1037–1054.

Enserink, M. (2011, November). Scientists brace for media storm around controversial flu studies. *ScienceInsider*. (Online).

Fanelli, D. (2009). How many scientists fabricate and falsify research? A systematic review and meta-analysis of survey data. *PLoS ONE*, 4(5): e5738.

Finholt, T.A. (2003). Collaboratories as a new form of scientific organization. *Economics of Innovation and New Technology*, 12(1), 5–25.

Gurstein, M. (2011). Evolving relationships: Universities, researchers and communities. *The Journal of Community Informatics*, 7(3). (Online).

Jackson, R. (1999). The universities, government and society. In D.C. Smith & A.K. Langslow (Eds.), *The Idea of a University* (pp. 91–105). London: Jessica Kingsley Publishers.

Jaschik, S. (2012, January). Humanities scholars consider the role of peer review. *Inside Higher Ed*. (Online).

Jones, D.R. (1999). Review of "Olaf Pedersen (1998), The first universities: studium generale and the origins of university education in Europe". *History of Education Quarterly*, 39(3), 363–365.

Jordan, B. (1989). *The Common Good: Citizenship, Morality and Self-Interest*. Oxford: Basil Blackwell.

Kavanaugh, A.L., Reese, D.D., Carroll, J.M., & Rosson, M.B. (2005). Weak ties in networked communities. *The Information Society*, 21(2), 119–131.

Kenzior, S. (2012, August 20). The Closing of American Academia. *Al Jazeera*. (Online).

Leavy, P. (2011). *Essentials of Transdisciplinary Research: Using Problem-Centered Methodologies*. Walnut Creek, CA: Left Coast Press.

Levelt Committee, Noort Committee, & Drenth Committee. (2012). Flawed science: The fraudulent research practices of social psychologist Diederik Stapel. Retrieved from http://www.tilburguniversity.edu/nl/nieuws-en-agenda/finalreportLevelt.pdf.

Leydesdorff, L., & Ward, J. (2005). Science shops: A kaleidoscope of science–society collaborations in Europe. *Public Understanding of Science, 14*(4), 353–372.

Loving, K., Stoecker, R., & Reddy, M. (2011). Service-learning, technology, nonprofits, and institutional limitations. In M. A. Bowdon & R. G. Carpenter (Eds.), *Higher Education, Emerging Technologies, and Community Partnerships: Concepts. Models, and Practices* (pp. 129–139). Hershey, PA: IGI.

MacLellan, M., & Talpalaru, M. (Eds.) (2012). *Remaking the Commons. Reviews in Cultural Theory, 2*(3), 1–6.

Manlow, V., Friedman, H., & Friedman, L. (2010). Inventing the future: Using the new media to transform a university from a teaching organization to a learning organization. *Journal of Interactive Learning Research, 21*(1), 47–64.

Mulgan, G. (2007). *Social Innovation: What Is It, Why It Matters, How It Can Be Accelerated.* London: The Young Foundation.

National Science Board (NSB) (2012). Trends and challenges for public research universities: Diminishing funding and rising expectations. Arlington, VA: National Science Board.

Nussbaum, M. C. (2010). *Not For Profit: Why Democracy Needs the Humanities.* Princeton, NJ: Princeton University Press.

Payne, S.L., & Calton, J.M. (2004). Exploring research potentials and applications for multi-stakeholder learning dialogues. *Journal of Business Ethics, 55*(1), 71–78.

Preece, J., & Shneiderman, B. (2009). The reader-to-leader framework: Motivating technology-mediated social participation. *AIS Transactions on Human-Computer Interaction, 1*(1), 13–32.

Sample, I. (2012, July 15). Free access to British scientific research within two years. *The Guardian.* (Online).

Schuler, D. (2008). *Liberating Voices: A Pattern Language for Communication Revolution.* Cambridge, MA: MIT Press.

Scott, A.O. (2010, October 8). Review of "Inside Job": Who maimed the economy, and how. *The New York Times.* (Online).

Spyns, P., de Moor, A., Vandenbussche, J., & Meersman, R. (2006). From folksologies to ontologies: How the twain meet. In R. Meersman & Z. Tari (Eds.), *On the Move to Meaningful Internet Systems 2006: CoopIS, DOA, GADA, and ODBASE* (pp. 738–755). Berlin: Springer.

Stoecker, R. (2008). Challenging institutional barriers to community-based research. *Action Research, 6*(1), 49–67.

Strand, K.J., Cutforth, N., Stoecker, R., Marullo, S., & Donohue, P. (2003). *Community-Based Research and Higher Education: Principles and Practices* (1st ed.). San Francisco, CA: Jossey-Bass.

Taylor, M.C. (2009, April 27). End the university as we know it. *The New York Times.* (Online).

Upbin, B. (2013, March 1). PatientsLikeMe is building a self-learning healthcare system. *Forbes Magazine.* (Online).

West, J., & Lakhani, K.R. (2008). Getting clear about communities in open innovation. *Industry & Innovation, 15*(2), 223–231.

Williamson, A., & DeSouza, R. (Eds.) (2007). *Researching with Communities: Grounded Perspectives on Engaging Communities in Research.* Auckland: Muddycreekpress.

Yapa, L. (2009). Transforming the university through community engagement. *Journal of Higher Education Outreach and Engagement, 13*(3), 131–146.

Chapter 6

WHAT'S SO SPECIAL ABOUT THE MOBILE PHONE?

Exploring the mobile phone as a legacy of its ICT progenitors

JANE VINCENT

The use of mobile phones in society for business, social networking and always-available connectivity has conflated the capabilities of its progenitors into a single device in a way like no other previous technology. This chapter explores the legacy information and communications technologies that preceded the mobile phone and examines the ways that they may have contributed to the special place that mobile phones have in everyday contemporary society. It is illustrated by examples from the UK, taken from the author's 12 years of published research about ICT users, from her family history, and her employment in mobile communications industries. Concepts of domestication and electronic emotion are used to explicate the discussion which posits that progenitor technologies are continuing to influence and shape the dynamic and ongoing domestication of mobile phones, as well as the smartphones and tablets now being introduced. The convergence of the capabilities that have supported the social interaction of people in business and society for over a century into this single device does, indeed, appear to make the mobile phone an extraordinary and special device.

Introduction

The mobile phone is probably the most used of all information and communication technologies (ICTs) (ITU 2010, 2012, Vincent 2006, 2010), and perhaps also the one that elicits the most emotional reaction about both its use and its impact on private and public space (Vincent 2011a, Höflich 2009). In this chapter I examine some of the ways in which the electronic emotions (Vincent & Fortunati 2009) encountered in contemporary everyday social practices of mobile phone use may have derived from our prior and contemporaneous use of communications technologies (telegraph, telephone, camera, projector, telex, computer/laptop) going back some 170 years. The chapter explores how people have managed their everyday communications through the development of information communication technologies (ICTs) over time. It then draws on the concepts of domestication (Silverstone & Hirsch 1992, Silverstone & Haddon 1996), and electronic emotion (Fortunati & Vincent 2009, Fortunati 2009), to follow the technological and social developments that have led to the present day ubiquitous presence of mobile phones in everyday life. Primary research conducted over a period of ten years examining mobile phone use in the UK is used for contemporary exemplars, as well as examples from my personal experiences of working in telecommunications industries. Secondary research from telecommunications and family history archives is used to illustrate the legacy systems from which the mobile phone has emerged. These illustrations are mostly taken from UK and British experiences. The chapter begins by examining the context of the legacy communications systems that preceded mobile phone development illustrated by examples of various user experiences. Adopting new technologies has been explored extensively by others in many disciplines including science and technologies studies such as Grint and Woolgar (1997), and Bijker and Law (1992). The historical work of Marvin (1988) also gives a hint of what life was like when electric communications were new, creating excitement (and some fear) among people encountering electricity for the first time. Indeed, the social history of technologies is represented by such a variety of research that I can only glance at it here (McLuhan 1964, de sola Pool 1977, Standage 1998, Pacey 1999). Thus I focus on what has made the mobile phone apparently such a special ICT in contemporary society.

Telegrams and tubes

The telegram sent via the telegraph service became increasingly important for local communications in mid-to-late 19th century. Telegraph wire systems and bicycle couriers struggled to keep up with demand for the delivery of messages, particularly in cities with stock exchanges and a high level of business transactions. Many of the larger cities, including London, New York, Berlin, Prague and Liverpool, introduced a network of pneumatic tubes through which messages could be sent at high speed (Standage 1998). This allowed them to arrive in times only exceeded today by instantaneous email and text messaging. Personal messages were also sent via pneumatic tubes from especially built Telegraph Offices such as in the premises I had the task of managing in 1981 while working for British Telecom. A declining 19th century building in Liverpool, Telegraph House still contained the long unused telegraph office built when the pneumatic system was at its height of popularity. The office had remained intact with its polished mahogany desk, elegant brass tubes and high-class fittings that far exceeded the quality of the 1980s Post Office counters. Going to the Telegraph Office was an event and the splendour of the establishment still showed through the dust of decades of neglect. Some of the mystique of this system is conveyed also in Truffaut's 1968 film *Stolen Kisses*[1] in which a message is shown moving along the pneumatic tube system in Paris as a symbol of the spirit passing between and uniting two lovers. Be it the cycle courier, the pneumatic tube, the short message system or some other means of ICT conveying the message, this part of the journey links the space between the sender and recipient, and assuring successful delivery is paramount. Whereas today text messages may be lost due to lack of memory capacity in the receiving device or an occasional cellular network problem, the vagaries of the pneumatic system meant that messages stuck in the tube had to be located and then accessed via tunnels or even digging up the road to release them.

> Ultimately, the pneumatic tubes' impracticalities, limitations, and economic unfeasibility led to its "death" as a medium, though it still lies dormant underneath city streets worldwide.[2]

It is notable that once the voice telephone system began to be introduced, providing valuable audible communication between those who were apart, it further diminished the need for such extensive telegraph services. The telephone immediately extended the reach of real time synchronous communications – although ironically it eventually lead to voice mail and other recorded messaging services and the return to asymmetrical communications.

Projectors and phonographs

The enthusiasm that we see today for the latest mobile phone technology such as smartphone apps was certainly matched in the past by the enthusiasm for the latest technologies. Such experiences included attending the telegraph office to see one's personal telegraph transmitted by pneumatic tube or going to public events where new technologies formed part of the entertainment experience. Some 120 or so years ago the challenges of using technology

---

[1]   http://www.youtube.com/watch?v=YLEJbFKTyQIExcerptshowingpneumatictube systemfromStolenKisses (accessed 11 January 2013).

[2]   http://cultureandcommunication.org/deadmedia/index.php/Pneumatic_Tubes Ghastly remnants of a dead medium (accessed 11 January 2013).

to illustrate a public talk could be fraught with some technical difficulties that nevertheless enhanced the public's wonderment. My great-grandfather was a regular speaker in London's public halls to Band of Hope (Methodist temperance league) meetings and, supported by his son, he used an oxy-hydrogen[3] lantern slide projector. The light for the projector was produced by the mixing of oxygen and hydrogen gases to provide the most powerful and most brilliant of limelight configurations because it had the hottest flame. However, because the gases were mixed before the point of combustion it was also the most dangerous, requiring great care in its operation, needing to be adjusted by the projectionist every minute or so; should there be an error there was risk of explosion. When the phonograph was invented, that too was incorporated into my great-grandfather's talks, as noted by his son William.

> During these years (the late 19th century) the phonograph came into being and one was brought [*sic*] for the firm which my father could always borrow, how well do I remember those sound wax cylinders & how careful one had to be with them, one day someone over balanced the case & bang went about a £1 worth of records. What a nasal twang those Yankee announcers had, what a paraphernalia that was to carry about, a large case for the wax cylinders – the instrument itself – a big stand to support the very large horn. Well many a happy hour we had with those Edison Bell records for in those days such instruments were not found in every house. (Dr William Vincent, 1886–1931).[4]

The fragility of wax cylinders mean few survived but some recording a family Christmas in 1904 have recently been rediscovered and made available to the BBC.[5] They thank the hosts and mark the event with a cheer and a message for posterity.

The development of visual aids for presentation purposes has continued apace with the advent of computer-based systems and perhaps Microsoft Power Point being a major turning point in style and method. The use of images to support, or replace, textual data has become particularly popular in the second decade of the 21st century as convergence of ICT capabilities allows for greater ease of access and transfer of photographs to presentation material, as well as within text messages and emails.

---

[3] http://www.artgallery.sa.gov.au/noye/Lantern/Lighting.htm Art Gallery of South Australia, Sources of Light for Magic Lanterns (accessed 12 January 2012).

[4] http://www.vincents.org.uk/archives/302 (accessed 29 August 2011).

[5] http://www.bbc.co.uk/news/science-environment-20774278.

Picture cards and text messages

The use of photographic portraits to send messages began almost as soon as photography was invented. They have developed from studio-based images taken by professionals in the 19th century to snapshots taken on pocket cameras and shared on digital social media today. During visits to seaside resorts such as Brighton in the early 20th century family portraits were taken by "roving" photographers and posted home as a postcard (Vincent 2012). Nowadays, even the pocket camera is becoming obsolete as the omnipresent smartphones and camera phones enable photographs to be recorded and immediately sent to recipients throughout the globe. Our excitement with technology continued with the development of the camera and photography and for a while the collections of *cartes de visite* (portrait photo visiting cards) became quite the vogue in early 20th century England (Sarvas & Frohlich 2011), as well as collecting post cards. The text which follows is from a 1907 example from a Vincent family album.

> Dear Will, Another card for your collection. How many have you now. I have about 250 Goodbye for the present with love to all from Alice (Vincent Family Album)

A century later and people were collecting phone cards (prepaid cards for use in public payphones), and now even mobile phones are collected. The saving of objects for nostalgic and emotional reasons is an age-old phenomenon. Following Harper (2002) and his research on photo elicitation, it would appear that people with common interests find something special in collecting, retrieving and sharing their artefact.

Photographs appear to capture the impossible: a person gone; an event past. That extraordinary sense of seeming to retrieve something that has disappeared belongs alone to the photographs, and it leads to deep and interesting talk (Harper 2002, p. 23).

Harper's enthusiastic description of photographs is, I suggest, also applicable to the postcards, text messages and mobile phones, all of which draw out visual memories via photos and text about things that people hold dear to their self. Numerous respondents in my research have kept old mobile phones, some because of the messages and contact details they hold from deceased friends and relatives, others because of photos associated with their children or for nostalgic reasons associated with the emotional memories engendered by the device. One mother explained how her daughter had refused to pass on her mobile phone to her younger brother:

We'd agreed she'd give her old phones to her younger brother; I found out later that she hadn't been doing this but had been keeping them under her pillow – she couldn't bear to think of her brother using them. (Vincent 2005, p. 224)

The sending of written messages instead of, or as well as, photographs was significantly augmented with the availability of mobile phone texting. Early enthusiasts who discovered short message service (SMS) as a complement to voice calls in the mid-1990s led the rapid take up of this service (Taylor & Vincent 2005, Goggin 2006, Hillebrand et al. 2010). 115 billion text messages were sent in the UK alone in 2011 but they are now being replaced by instant messaging, Twitter, Instagram, email, or messaging and shared Apps between proprietary smartphone/tablets such as via the popular Apple, Samsung and Blackberry devices.

Fixed line and mobile phones

The fixed line telephone, present in almost every UK household today, was slow to be adopted after its introduction in the late 19th century, only gaining momentum after it was nationalised and run by the Post Office in 1912 (Perry 1977). Similar to the mobile phone, fixed phones were initially used by businesses and wealthier private customers, but it took time for it to complement and supersede the popular, competitively priced, telegram and postal services. Commercial mobile telephone services first appeared as radio car telephones in the 1960s and these stayed in use until the late 1980s in the UK. Early cellular mobile phones partly replicated these car phones as the mobile phone was seen as an adjunct to private transport mobility and so was largely provided for use in cars, and other vehicles. Early handheld devices were bulky and not very portable, but nevertheless they quickly became a compelling "must have" device, most notably by young urban professionals of the 1980s, and mobile phone growth outpaced business predictions year on year. Interestingly, both fixed line and mobile phone services were initially implemented by private companies in a competitive market. However, early capital investment in the fixed telephone service was inadequate, and the tariffs were not competitive; the mobile phone network operators, on the other hand, provided a greater depth of coverage and driven by customer demand for mobile phones they were able to offer a quality of service at an acceptable price to their customers.

Similar concerns were expressed about both fixed and mobile telephones with regard to possible detrimental effects on health, as well as with regard to its impact on the household and everyday life. It was at first suggested that using a fixed telephone might drive people insane. People feared they might be infected by disease transmitted over the phone line or even get electric shocks (Marvin 1988, p. 132). Risks associated with the use of mobile phones by their users include health concerns regarding microwaves from the phones and masts, as well accident hazards arising from walking or driving whilst using a mobile phone.

The emotional response to the phone was not confined to health matters. The fixed telephone was initially seen as a device that was for emergencies in particular, and this combined with the "cheaper after 6pm" tariff shaped the ways that fixed and even mobile phones were used for many years. The ringing of a telephone was not to be tolerated – it had to be answered. Fixed-line voicemail devices were not in common use for many decades and it often fell to the women (or staff) of the household to deal with incoming calls. Conversations with my own family members who remembered the phone arriving in their house in the 1920s and 1930s said that their mothers complained of the emotional upset the phone caused as they had to deal with other people's problems in the privacy of their own home. It also tied them to the house as they were expected to be there all the time in case an urgent call was received. This was in complete contrast with the experiences of some respondents of my mobile phone studies who said how much more freedom they had after they bought a mobile phone: *"I love it because we are not restricted"* (Vincent 2005, p. 222).

The traditional fixed telephone is now being removed, or not installed, in some businesses and households, to be replaced by mobile phones and Internet based communications. However, the legacy of telephones being the "always on" and primary means for emergency contact prevails and as overarching theme.

Emotional tensions between ICTs

It would seem that new contemporary technology, whether it is in the 19th, 20th, or 21st century, evokes a strong, often enthusiastic, emotional response to using new devices, as well as being linked to the emotions involved in the presentation of oneself to others. For example, witness the widespread phenomenon of supplementing talking with additional visual material that is shared and shown off via the mobile phone (Vincent 2009, 2012). Furthermore, the shared enthusiasm among the audience who are partaking in the experience is somehow enriched by the modernist way it is presented. The tension and anticipation of the gas limelight of the 1890s is not so dissimilar to those moments when we rediscover a photograph or video clip on the Internet, anticipate the arrival of a new smartphone or wait for an audio visual presentation to commence only to find the Mac is not compatible with the projector and it does not work. Indeed, the tension associated with using novel devices was also experienced by a respondent I interviewed when he first used a mobile phone in public:

> The first phone call I made on a hand portable was on Holborn Viaduct Railway station… which was Easter 1985. And I made a call to tell my wife I was coming home by a certain time. She was at home as a, a housewife. I was looked upon by people on the station, carrying this £3000 Motorola 8000X brick as if I was somebody who lived on another planet. So in those days, if you made a phone call out in the street or on a train or a bus you were considered to be very strange. (Vincent 2010, p. 161)

Communications, of course, are not simply limited to the passing of information between parties or to conversations but can achieved through shared experiences such as leisure pursuits. Devices and games that enable the ludic qualities of interaction as well as (for some) more serious pastimes such as playing chess have transferred easily to computational devices. However, although electronic devices do enable many modes of communication, including games, there are, of course, many people who still like and love more traditional ways of doing things such as using a manual typewriter or a fountain pen and paper (Fortunati & Vincent 2012). They may seek the nostalgia of old telephones, like to play board games, or develop their own 35mm film with all the chemistry that it involves. Nevertheless, many people have also moved on and instead, or as well as, using these older methods prefer their mobile phone, complemented by other more specialist ICT devices such as a digital SLR camera.

Discussion and concluding remarks

It would appear from this brief examination of some of the legacy systems of the mobile phone that there has been a largely linear development of information and communications technologies over 170 years. The examples given in Table 6.1 show some major turning points with these ICTs, including developments in mobile phones themselves. The notion that we have only used sound and image to communicate since technologies such as the telegraph and the camera were invented is, of course, erroneous for humans have creatively used all kinds of artefacts to convey messages. However, returning to the question being explored here, that of the ICT progenitors of the mobile phone I would argue that it owes its legacy mostly to the developing telecommunications and computer science industry – supported by the electricity and power capabilities that are needed to make them work.

Table 6.1. Suggested progenitors for the mobile phone[6]

ICT	Date first used
Photograph	1825
Telegraph	1838
Private telegraph service	1851
Voice telephone	1877
Portable limelight projectors	1888
Telegraphone/answerphone	1902
Mobile phone/hand held	1946/1973
World Wide Web	1989
Digital mobile phones/international roaming	1991
Short message service texts	1992
Featurephones	1999
Smartphones	2007

Over this 170-year period we have amassed numerous communications modes and technologies among which are those that gave us snapshot images; notes, text messages and emails; telephony; broadcast radio and television, music and games. Each of these is integral to developing and maintaining interaction within and between communities as well the personal and family needs they sustain. Today we still use cameras, write letters, have face-to-face conversations and play board games but we can also do all of these on our mobile phone as well as via other individual devices designed for the specific task. Nowadays we communicate and play with electronic computational devices, whereas in the past we would have just waited until we could speak to each other directly or sent messages via others. Looking back in time at some of the old ways we did things that today we take for granted does, however, highlight some intriguing similarities in our emotional responses and perhaps may in some way account for our present social practices. These are the activities that, as we

---

[6] As smartphones and mobile devices become more inclusive television, radio, micro-payment systems, computer games, mobile phone Apps, and more can be added to this list. However, to some extent these could be considered as 'add-on', or OTT, over the top technologies, which require the basic mobile phone capability to function.

have already learned from our forebears, are so domesticated within our daily lives that we take them for granted. At one time every one of these activities, technologies or devices, was a new idea, an innovation of its time; some found a niche and then died away and others grew and developed and improved. I would suggest it is because of this longitudinal development and growth of communications social practices and the emotions that are implicitly associated with them that the mobile phone has become such a highly charged emotional communications compendium. It is an almost unique sum of all types of electronic and mechanical communication, computational games, social networking, photographic presentation of the self, audio recordings and more.

Thus, the assertion that the mobile phone is in some way the contemporary apotheosis of communications technologies and electronic emotions requires further examination. Let us consider first how the mobile phone has come to supplant and complement multiple individual ICTs: I turn firstly to the work of Silverstone and Hirsch (1992) on domestication and then to my work with Leopoldina Fortunati (Vincent & Fortunati 2009, Fortunati 2009) on electronic emotions. Domestication as a concept originated from anthropology, consumption studies and modern media studies (Silverstone & Haddon 1996) and refers to the way that people eventually adopt and incorporate technologies (and ideas) into their everyday home life. Silverstone revisited this concept some years later suggesting that the process involves the "constant renegotiation" of values and boundaries with regard to privacy and proximity in particular (Silverstone 2006, p. 233). Indeed, over the decades radio broadcasts, television, and telephones have come to be accepted as part of everyday life, but when they were first made available they elicited all types of emotion responses such as delight, derision, fear and fascination (Marvin 1988, Lasén, 2005). The emotion being expressed (or felt inwardly) with regard to using these different devices was thus not a response to the social practice of communicating but rather was the response to the *modus operandi* being adopted for achieving new ways of doing old things. For example, receiving a phone call on a mobile phone in any location, even abroad, creates positive and negative responses from numerous respondents in my various studies such as in this example from Nigel, talking about using his phone when he was staying at his holiday home abroad.

If there's been a rugby game I'll ring one of my rugby mates and we'll talk about it, and last year during the world cup, er it was a way of releasing the emotional tension after a world cup game and I'd often ring my mate in England who'd been watching on it TV and we'd talk about it for 5 or 10 minutes just so that I'd, just sort of, just get back on an even keel. (Vincent 2011b, p. 134)

In our research on emotions in the social practices of ICT users (Vincent & Harper 2003, Vincent & Haddon 2004, Vincent & Fortunati 2009) it was found that people of all ages were drawn to use communications technologies – and in particular the mobile phone – because they enabled them to easily maintain their emotional ties to friends, family and work. These relationships engendered "electronic emotions" – the emotions lived, re-lived or discovered through machines (Fortunati & Vincent 2009, p. 13). Electronic emotions help shape the way mobile phones (and other ICTs) are used and in turn influence the design and availability of new products and services. For example, the alacrity with which people adopted short message service and their subsequent zealous use of texting, leading to dependence[7] and even addiction for some, highlights the emotion associated with just one of the mobile phone's capabilities. Furthermore, whilst the type of device, the technology or the applications used are very important for some, it appears that most people acquire a particular brand or model of mobile phone because of their affiliations, their peer group influences and their relevance to what they do in their day to day life. However, although there is evidence of these electronic emotions in the everyday uses of the device (Vincent 2009, Sugiyama 2009) it is not apparent why mobile phones in particular have become so much more imbued with emotion than other electronic computational communications devices. Carried everywhere and used at inappropriate moments, they are the first thing people grab in a crisis to call a loved one for emotional support (Rimé 2009, Vincent 2011a, b). This is further exemplified in the powerful accounts of last words with loved ones in terror attacks (Dutton & Nainoa 2002). As I have explored the puzzle of mobile phone use in my research it has become clear to me that for most users it is much more than just a device for communicating and storing data. Furthermore, people do seem to desire particular models of phone that they can customise to their personal needs as well as it being representative of their identity. That the device itself creates an emotional response is not unexpected (Norman 2004) but what appears unique to the mobile phone is that this emotion is

---

[7]   http://withoutmedia.wordpress.com/ Study by University of Maryland ICMPA 2010 (accessed 9 September 2011).

in some way enhanced by everything it contains – each phone having been uniquely modified by its user.

The curious fact is that although the mobile phone does do all these things in one tiny hand-held gadget it has not supplanted the projector, camera, audio recorder, telephone, television, radio, music player, photo album, games console, phone directory and address book. Instead it has become a shortcut, a shorthand compendium comprising all these capabilities, often used as a temporary (location-based) substitute to be replaced by the real thing such as the projector, the PC, or a paper-based address book when this function is the primary lead technological device most suited for that occasion.

Understanding more about the domestication process of each legacy system as well as the accumulation of the electronic emotions that are associated with these communications experiences are, I suggest, the key to beginning to unlock the mystery of our affection for mobiles. It appears the mobile phone is not only imbued with the social practices surrounding these numerous communications media but it is also imbued with the legacy systems from which they are derived, and the synthesis of the domestication processes that these have entailed. In turn, our mobile phones of the last 20 years are themselves now being conflated with a new generation of smartphones, tablets, and mobile operating systems that offer access to a greater variety of mobile applications than ever before.

In this chapter I have explored how communications technologies have followed both individual developmental and domestication progressions as well as combining multiple technologies through convergence to be available on a single device: the mobile phone. Concurrent with the domestication has been the development of strong electronic emotions with regard to the mobile phone, and it is these electronic emotions that have considerable influence on the choice and uses of ICTs. I have illustrated the chapter with my research findings with regard to the mediation of emotion as well as examining the progenitors of the mobile phone – particularly the camera, telegraph, telephone and text. What this has highlighted is that there has been a constant and dynamic domestication of communication technologies, the sum of which are contained in the mobile phone. In sum, it would appear that people use their mobile phone extensively to manage and mediate emotions with regard to the highs and lows of their self, their relationships and family commitments. Furthermore the mobile phone has incorporated, but not necessarily replaced, other domesticated technologies with which it still interacts or combines. Mobile phones (and the new smartphone and tablet devices) have won a special place in the lives of many people in the UK and beyond; these individually personalised compendiums of everyday life show no sign of being displaced.

References

Bijker, W.E., & Law, J. (Eds.) (1992). *Shaping Technology/Building Society.* Cambridge: MIT Press.

de Sola Pool, I. (Ed.) (1977). *The Social Impact of the Telephone.* Cambridge: MIT Press.

Dutton, W., & Nainoa, F. (2002). Say goodbye… let's roll: The social dynamics of wireless networks on September, 11th. *Prometheus 20*(3), 237–245.

Fortunati, L. (2009). Theories without heart. In A. Esposito & R. Vich (Eds.), *Cross Modal Analysis of Speech, Gestures, Gaze and Facial Expression.* COST Action 2012 International Conference, Prague, Czech Republic, October 15–18 2008, Revised, Selected and Invited papers, Lecture Notes in Computer Science 5641 (pp. 5–17). London: Springer.

Fortunati, L., & Vincent, J. (2009). Introduction. In J. Vincent & L. Fortunati (Eds.), *Electronic Emotion: The Mediation of Emotion via Information and Communication Technologies* (pp. 1–34). Oxford: Peter Lang.

Fortunati, L., & Vincent, J. (2012). Have our communications become more sensorial and emotionally intense with the growth of multimodal communications media? Paper presented at Internet Research 13.0: Technologies, The 13th Annual International and Interdisciplinary Conference of the Association of Internet Researchers (AoIR), 18–21 October 2012.

Goggin, G. (2006). *Cell Phone Culture: Mobile Technology in Everyday Life.* London: Routledge.

Grint, R., & Woolgar, S. (1997). *The Machine at Work: Technology Work and Organization.* Oxford: Polity Press

Harper, D. (2002). Talking about Pictures: A case for photo elicitation. *Visual Studies, 17*(1), 13–26.

Hillebrand, F., Trosby, F., Holley, K., & Harris, I. (Eds.) (2010). *Short Message Service (SMS): The Creation of Personal Global Text Messaging.* Chichester: Wiley.

Höflich, J. (2009). Mobile phone calls and emotional stress. In L. Vincent. & L. Fortunati (Eds.), *Electronic Emotion: The Mediation of Emotion via Information and Communication Technologies* (pp. 63–84). Oxford: Peter Lang.

ITU. (2010). *The World in 2010 ICT Facts and Figures, Report by the Market Information and Statistics Division.* Geneva: Telecommunication Development Bureau.

ITU. (2012). *Measuring the Information Society.* Geneva: Telecommunication Development Bureau.

Lasén, A. (2005). The social shaping of fixed and mobile networks: A historical comparison. In P. Gossett. (Ed.), *Understanding Mobile Phone Users and Usage* (pp. 1–43). Newbury: Vodafone Group.

Marvin, C. (1988). *When Old Technologies Were New. Thinking about Electric Communication in the Late Nineteenth Century.* New York: Oxford University Press.

McLuhan, M. (1964). *Understanding Media: The Extensions of Man.* New York: McGraw-Hill.

Norman, D. (2004). *Emotional Design: Why We Love (Or Hate) Everyday Things.* New York: Basic Books.

Pacey, A. (1999). *Meaning in Technology.* Cambridge Mass. MIT Press.

Perry, C.R. (1977). The British experience. In I. de Sola Pool (Ed.), *The Social Impact of the Telephone* (pp. 69–96). Cambridge: MIT Press.

Rimé, B. (2009). Emotion elicits the social sharing of emotion. *Emotion Review 1*, 60–85.

Sarvas, R., & Frohlich, D. (2011). *From Snapshots to Social Media: The Changing Picture of Domestic Photography*. London: Springer Verlag.

Silverstone, R. (2006). Reflections on the life of a concept. In T. Berker, M. Hartmann, Y. Punie, & K. Ward (Eds.), *Domestication of Media and Technology* (pp. 229–248). Maidenhead: Open University Press.

Silverstone, R., & Haddon, L. (1996). Design and the domestication of information and communication technologies: Technical change and everyday life. In R. Silverstone & R. Mansell (Eds.), *Communication by Design: The Politics of Information and Communication Technologies* (pp. 44–74). Oxford: Oxford University Press.

Silverstone, R., & Hirsch, E. (Eds.). (1992). *Consuming Technologies: Media and Information in Domestic Spaces*. London: Routledge.

Standage, T. (1998). *The Victorian Internet: The Remarkable Story of the Telegraph and the Nineteenth Century's Online Pioneers*. London: Weidenfeld and Nicholson.

Sugyama, S. (2009). Decorated mobile phones and emotional attachment for Japanese youths. In J. Vincent & L. Fortunati (Eds.), *Electronic Emotion: The Mediation of Emotion via Information and Communication Technologies* (pp. 85–103). Oxford: Peter Lang.

Taylor, A.S., & Vincent, J. (2005). An SMS history. In L. Hamill &, A. Lasén (Eds.), *Mobile World Past, Present and Future* (pp. 75–92). London: Springer.

Vincent, J. (2005). Are people affected by their attachment to their mobile phone? In K. Nyiri, (Ed.) *A Sense of Place: The Global and the Local in Mobile Communication* (pp. 221–229). Vienna: Passagen Verlag.

Vincent, J. (2006). Emotional attachment and mobile phones. *Knowledge Technology and Policy, 19*, 29–44.

Vincent, J. (2009). Affiliations, emotion and the mobile phone. In A. Esposito & R. Vích (Eds.), *Cross-Modal Analysis of Speech, Gestures, Gaze and Facial Expression: COST Action 2012 International Conference, Prague, Czech Republic, October 15–18, 2008 Revised Selected and Invited Papers* (pp. 28–41). Berlin: Springer Verlag.

Vincent, J. (2010). Living with mobile phones. In J.R. Höflich, G.F. Kircher, C. Linke & I. Schlote (Eds.), *Mobile Media and the Change of Everyday Life* (pp. 155–170). Frankfurt am Main: Peter Lang.

Vincent, J. (2011a). Emotion and the mobile phone. In H. Greif, L. Hjorth, A. Lasén & C. Lobet-Maris (Eds.), *Cultures of Participation Media Practices, Politics and Literacy* (pp. 99–110). Berlin: Peter Lang.

Vincent, J. (2011b). *Emotion in the Social Practices of Mobile Phone Users*. Doctoral Thesis, University of Surrey.

Vincent, J. (2012). Mediating emotions via visual communications: An exploration of the visual presentation of self via mobile phones. In A. Benedek & K. Nyír (Eds.), *Visual Learning, Vol. 2: The Iconic Turn in Education* (pp. 85–96). Frankfurt: Peter Lang Verlag.

Vincent, J. & Fortunati, L. (2009). (Eds.) *Electronic Emotion: The Mediation of Emotion via Information and Communication Technologies*. Oxford: Peter Lang.

Vincent, J. & Haddon, L. (2004). *Informing suppliers about user behaviours to better prepare them for the 3G/UMTS*. Customers Report 34 UMTS Forum. Guildford, UK: University of Surrey.

Vincent, J. & Harper, R. (2003). *Social shaping of UMTS. Preparing the 3G customer*. Report 26 UMTS Forum. Guildford, UK: University of Surrey.

Acknowledgements

This chapter was inspired by recently discovered family archives including reminiscences noted by a relative in the 1920s and made available online by Jeff Vincent. Acquiring the latest communications technology has been "in the family" for at least five generations and it appears enjoying new gadgets and gizmos continues as the family iPad in continual use, and the iPhone in my teenager's almost constant grasp will testify.

Chapter 7

UNDERSTANDING THE USE OF MOBILE PHONES IN DIFFICULT CIRCUMSTANCES

Larry Stillman

This chapter examines the concept of disruption through a speculative case study of the ICT interactions (particularly mobile phones) of low-income Africans on the urban fringe of Johannesburg. The chapter is intended to contribute to the development of a more politically conscious understanding of social-technological relations. The privileging of a "Northern" view of technology, viewed as positive disruption, operates at a remove from what can occur in the global South. Understanding technology in society is more than being sensitive to questions of design, use, adoption or adaptation in particular cultural, economic, political or social conditions. The analysis of such relations also needs to be judged politically. This then allows for a strong check on unreal aspirations for ICT-related change that does not take into account determining social forces.

Introduction

The mobile phone is now used by billions of users around the world. Consequently, it might appear self-evident that mobile phones do in fact "constitute the basis for one of the greatest expansions of human capabilities in known history" (Smith et al 2011). But the circumstances that result in the attraction and capability offered by mobile phones are very different for the very poor. The utility of the mobile as a communications device is the result of particular life conditions, and in this case, the attraction needs to be explained in the context of the overall state of pervasive disruption in the lives of low-income people. Thus while the mobile phone may be perceived by the slum dweller to provide a degree of comparative advantage, status and personal agency (all the subject of marketing campaigns by the telcos in South Africa), in the grand scheme of things, without more profound changes in society, the device of itself can do little to break the cycle of poverty and physical disability that the users find themselves in due to overarching historical circumstances. Hence, while the mobile phone and social media applications are increasingly important as a means of connecting people to social protest, whether in L'Aquila (as in this volume), or street protests in Cairo, the social forces against its users are still massive and their power should not be discounted – including the power to turn off connectivity (Spinks 2013).

Indeed, for some critics, the idea that the poor will be able to find their way out of poverty is contradicted by cold facts about the South African economy: "the structural trend runs in the opposite direction: toward re-ducing the size of [the] core of workers. Economic informality is growing in South Africa and it is irreversible: the traditional narrative of economic modernisation is running in reverse" (Marais 2011, p. 183). Consequently, one commentator has gone so far as to suggest that despite the widespread uptake of mobile phones by the poor "there is no hard evidence that there are fewer poorer people on the [African] continent as a result of access to ICTs" (Gillwald 2010, p. 80). The realities for what a mobile phone can provide are very different between the affluent global North and the poorer global South.

Drawing on critical theory and the desire for knowledge that leads to enlightenment and human emancipation (Bohman 2013, Habermas 1971), this chapter is consequently critical of the "myth of infinite benefit", familiar from the discourse of technological enthusiasts (Han 2012, citing Sarewitz, p. 2062). It uses research conducted with poor South Africans as a springboard for theorisation.

Topologically, we can see the mobile phone as a portable artefact em-bedded in socio-technical communicative arrangements that are "stretched" across time and space. Drawing on geographic (Dist 2009, Gren 2009) and structuration theory (Giddens 1984, Chapter 3), these communicative arrangements should be understood as taking place on a topologically "uneven" surface, reflecting people's different circumstances. From a critical theory perspective, poor people's lives are in the final analysis overwhelm-ingly conditioned by circumstances not always of their choosing, elements over which "that actor has neither helped to bring into being nor has any significant control over" (ibid, p. 346). Despite the tendency of capitalism to create a "smooth space defined by uncoded flows, flexibility, continual modulation, and tendential equalization" (Hardt & Negri 2000, p. 327), the result is often increased segmentation in the periphery, including the global South. Bourdieu has written that there are "objective structures which are independent of the consciousness and desires of agents and are capable of guiding or constraining their practices or their representations" (Bourdieu 1990, p. 123). These determining structures and conditions include such factors as poverty, disability, wealth, gender, or geographic location (Blackburn 1972), and they also set in place the "habitus", the sense of place a person has, as Bourdieu would put it (Bourdieu 1990, p. 131). The research background and following description of South Africa provides depth to such a viewpoint.

Background

Background to the chapter lies in research activity that has taken place since 2008 with the Digital Doorway Initiative (DDI), a project to provide public Internet terminals for the poorest people in South Africa. The DDI was initiated by the Meraka Institute of the South African Council for Scientific and Industrial Research as part of the Government of South Africa's strategic mandate for ICT development. The Digital Doorway kiosk is itself a multi-user terminal designed for unsupervised public use and is virtually indestructible. Several hundred kiosks have been installed in South Africa with others installed elsewhere in Africa. A related pilot project to use the Digital Doorway is now underway in remote indigenous communities in Australia. A key proposition of the DDI is that technology design, use, adoption and adaptation need to be understood as both products of, and embedded in, particular cultural and social conditions (Stillman et al. 2012). However, this chapter takes this proposition further, and embeds it in a more politicised understanding of the world.

There is also an ethical context to research by the DDI. Within the DDI there is concern about the role played by a researcher or technology specialist and effects of "interventions" intended to engender good or wellbeing, particularly when decisions are made without any effective community engagement. It is argued that ethical and effective interventions can be developed only through genuine partnerships with communities. Indeed, it always needs to be kept in mind that communities may in fact not want what is assumed to be good for them at all. Such a problematisation of assumptions about technology and international development is an unintended but important outcome in the thinking of the DDI over the past decade as well as other work in developing countries (Avgerou 2010).

Inequality and poverty in South Africa

How should poverty be defined? Poverty is not just a lack of physical resources, a job or cash, because a person can be financially very poor, but be very happy and socially connected. Poverty is a combination of physical conditions and the state of a person's being. Amartya Sen argues that "relationship between resources and poverty is both variable and deeply contingent on the characteristics of the respective people and the environment in which they live – both natural and social" (Sen 2009, p. 254). These factors include: gender, physical differences and disabilities; differences in the physical environment; variations in social climate (thus, the state of personal and public health); and relational perspectives, that is, the normative dimension associated with perceptions of dignity, poverty or disability, that is, the sense of honour or shame at one's state of affairs in the world.

In 2010, South Africa ranked 113th on the world's Human Development Index, just below Kyrgyzstan and above Syria.[1] Other than a small percentage of the population, the majority of South Africans are black, drawn from about 11 tribal groups, and poor and a third are very poor, assuming a poverty line of ZAR3,000, or about $AUD325 a year as of May 2013 (Chitiga-Mabugu 2013, p. 172). There are also the additional minorities of "coloured" mixed-race people (many of whom are poor), and the white Africans: mostly Afrikaners or English-speakers. Because of the vast inequalities in the distribution of wealth and infrastructure, policy-makers have labelled the country as a "developmental state" (Terreblanche 2009). Due to the historic compromises made in order to end apartheid, the African National Congress (ANC)-dominated government rejects nationalisation or even welfare state solutions to social problems. Individual initiative and subsequent wealth creation, rather than direct state intervention are seen as a solution to the problem of poverty (Marais 2011, Chapter 13).

The poorest households in South Africa are typically those headed by black women in rural areas, and AIDs or related conditions are widespread. South Africa is also increasingly urbanised, whether because of the deliberate policies of deracination under the apartheid regime, or the continuing massive wealth inequalities which exist in its neo-liberal economy today. Historically, residential divisions were used to reinforce racial divisions. The (black) poor were pushed to the city limits and segregated by the notorious pass laws which did not permit legal residence in white-only areas. Poor transport infrastructure kept physical movement slow, difficult and restricted for the

---

[1]   http://hdr.undp.org/en/reports/global/hdr2010 (accessed 1 September 2011).

majority of the population. This policy became known as the paradigmatic "Apartheid City", whose effects continue today (Schensul & Heller 2011). This results in what is known as "inside-out city form, with most of the poor located beyond the urban belt, at extreme distances and high densities in terms of international norms" (Cross 2013).

Millions of people now live in officially recognised settlements (such as Soweto), or more recent shanty towns (called informal settlements) such as Zandspruit, discussed in more detail below. The number of informal settlements has gone up from 300 in 1994 to over 2700 in 2011. People on the margins have a sense of being thrown away (Afrikaans *weggooimense*), according to one study of Cape Town slum dwellers, and this self-perception of urban refugees may well extend to other informal communities (Ross 2013, p. 454). Social and infrastructural problems (Hemson et al. 2008) continue with water, sanitation and garbage collection, power, and even traversable roads lacking in settlements. Protest riots are not at all infrequent due to the lack of government action and endemic corruption (Harber 2011, Huchzermeyer 2009).

It must be remembered that these constrictions are typical of the life of many urban poor throughout the world. Thus, the poor have fallen by the wayside as physical and social infrastructure privileges those who have resources. In fact, as Harvey argues, "while the technological, social, political and institutional context has changed quite radically since Engels's time, the aggregate effective (sic) condition has in many respects worsened" (Harvey 2000, p. 15), and hence the shanty town is not surprising but to be expected. Mike Davis puts his own interpretation on the problem: "The global growth of a vast informal proletariat, moreover, is a wholly original structural development unforeseen by either classical Marxism or modernisation pundits... a true global residuum lacking the strategic economic power of socialised labour, but massively concentrated in a shanty-town world encircling the fortified enclaves of the urban rich" (Davis 2004, p. 27).

Except for mobile phones, in townships and settlements or rural villages, privately owned ICTs such as computers or laptops are not a financial or practical proposition for the vast majority of people (cost, access to power/Internet, and theft). Because not all people are on the electricity grid, many people rely upon car batteries or recharging at local shops or garages for a few precious Rand. For those who need them and have the money to pay, Internet computers are available through Internet cafes (sometimes housed in recycled shipping containers) but, for the poor, this activity is a luxury, rather than a commonplace activity. As another indicator of ICT disadvantage, there are approximately 30,000 schools in the country, perhaps only 20% having more than one computer (Gush et al. 2004).

Anecdotally, it also appears that mobile phones are not objects to be displayed as status symbols or a symbolic safety beacon, in contrast to the practice in other affluent countries (for example, girls walking with their mobile prominently displayed). Mobile phones are also not devices to be displayed in the lanes or streets because of the ease of theft (Han 2012, p. 2067), the fact of which was experienced by the author in a robbery in broad daylight.

Methodological considerations

The writer proposed a small-scale and short-term case study,[2] to provide more background to the kind of work being conducted by the DDI in deprived communities. The data collected was almost entirely concerned with their experience with mobile phones, their life histories and their personal mobility.

In an ideal world, one would hope to be able to locate a representative sample of different types of residents over the long-term, with the hope of reflecting different viewpoints and experiences that could then come together to present a defensible argument, meeting Walsham's categories of authenticity, creditability and criticality – that is, "the way in which the text probes readers to consider their taken-for-granted ideas and beliefs" (Walsham 2006, pp. 325–6). But the circumstances of the pilot limited these three categories being fully developed in a number of ways. First, the funding only allowed for a very short working time with interviewees. Consequently, an ultimately opportunistic convenience sample with English-speaking students was organised by intermediaries familiar with the community. In fact, because of safety concerns, interviews were conducted on campus, rather than in the settlement itself. A case study approach (Mjøset 2001) was also chosen because there was no other means of easily obtaining the story of slum-dwellers for the writer: in such trying conditions, it is well-nigh impossible to adopt a positivist approach and construct a fool-proof methodology (if such exists) such as a scientific sample of slum-dwellers' experiences of technology, nor was it feasible for a white outsider to settle into the community for either the short or long-term without considerable

---

[2]   Monash Human Ethics Approval CF10/2759 - 2010001563.

acculturation and the building of trust, notwithstanding the issues of racial difference or personal safety.

There was another significant issue. There are profound differences between the researcher and the researched: a white middle-class Australian and black Africans living in trying circumstances. Inevitably, the details of life in poverty will come up with at times highly emotional stories involving family tragedy, structural poverty and the inevitable story of physical and psychological disruption and physical displacement that is the story of South Africa. I am sure that at times, details were just not forthcoming from people about their life history or material circumstances, because of a justifiable sense of pride and potential loss of face in front of an older white person. Thus interviewees may have played out particular roles to what they thought was expected or hidden particular things, and much as I wanted to probe some details, I restrained myself. Moreover, the question has to be asked: what right do I have in the first place to assume that I have any right to conduct such research? Major ethical questions arise and consequently, the limitations discussed here have to be kept in mind with respect to the adequacy of the speculations developed in the chapter given the use of a convenience sample.

Additionally, no assumptions can be made about there being the possibility of a way of capturing, as in experimental science, "perfect knowledge" of the life conditions of the people I spoke with. Thus, what I learned should be regarded as inspiring conceptual insight, rather than actually depicting a firm reality. Because of these qualifications, the chapter's observations can only be regarded as exploratory though intentionally problematising.

The majority of interviewees came from Zandspruit, an informal settlement at the intersection of main highways on the north-west fringes of Johannesburg. My own experience of being in an informal settlement has also been confined to short-term visits to Zandspruit and other similar places. Other interviewees came from nearby settlements. The population of Zandspruit is about 60,000 (the precise number is unknown), with a very high number of unemployed and very low-income unskilled people, single parent householders (predominantly women), living in shacks, representative of the internal migration of people from all parts of South Africa and other countries to find work in the city. "Foreigners" are sometimes seen as not belonging to "the community", resulting in dreadful violent incidents that are referred to as xenophobic riots. Zandspruit has also been of particular interest to Monash University South Africa because it is relatively close to its campus and, under the University's social justice strategy, Monash conducts educational and other outreach activities to its residents.

Seven of the interviewees were men, four women, living in Zandspruit and other informal settlements. Three other interviews were conducted with African staff employed by Meraka, in a related project in regional towns. A colleague also offered valued insider commentary, providing insight into African cultural values, beliefs, and patterns of behaviour (Mbiti 1969) that are recognisably different from the minority culture of whites (the culture most familiar to outsiders, particularly foreign white researchers).

With the consent of participants, semi-structured interviews of up to an hour long were recorded. Questions concerned family background and relationships, exposure to and use of technology in daily life. Notes were taken with a Livescribe pen, allowing for unobtrusive recording and note-taking. The strength of Livescribe is that the pen and special paper map to an audio file which allows easy cross-referencing back to aural data. Through recursive listening, transcription and précis–making, I was able to high-light key points, reduce the data, alert myself to emerging themes, and develop memos from the data. This technique was derived from Grounded Theory methods, though I did not engage in the full data management and theory development process suggested. However, with the insight of Grounded Theory, I also hoped that the stories provided an inspiration to theory building and critique (Charmaz 2005, Glaser & Strauss 1967). I also shared my notes with the interviewees for comment, though very few changes were subsequently made.

I came to the case study with no set assumptions in mind about what the data might theoretically demonstrate, and I believe that this allowed me to be open to being challenged by the implications of what they said then locating relevant theories that I was comfortable with and provided insight to me (Walsham 2006, p. 325). I also worked with the assumption, based on Giddens' theories, that they were "experts" in describing their everyday life (Giddens 1984, p. 133). Furthermore, since the time of the original research I have become increasingly interested in the double hermeneutic – the form of discourse used by the research subject and the way in which it is re-expressed by researchers which can result in self-reflection that in turn effects future research, research discourse, and research relationships that follow. As Giddens has suggested, "all sociological research has a necessarily cultural, ethnographic or anthropological aspect to it" (Giddens, 1984, p. 284). Neither the complexity of intra-cultural "performances", "presentations of self" (Goffman 1971), nor the other's point of view should be underestimated

(Geertz 1973, Chapter 3). Thus, despite Walsham's suggestion that it is generally possible to break the ice in the interview (Walsham 2006, p. 323), for my own part, I was well aware of the inequality in the relationship and how this might constrain and distort interaction.

Other experiences since the time of the original research have also contributed to refining the theory development. First, an earlier form of the chapter was presented at a workshop at the Prato CIRN Community Informatics Conference in 2011, and the discussion it engendered was taken into account. Furthermore, the chapter's reviewers offered considerable additional insight. Third, several more visits to South Africa have added depth to an understanding of the place of ICTs in that society, as has further reading of research literature about South Africa and development. As Stake has suggested, "we see data sometimes pre-coded but continuously reinterpreted, on first encounter and again and again... An observation is interpreted against one issue, perspective or utility, then interpreted against others" (Stake 2005, p. 450).

The concept of disruption

There are a number of ways in which disruption can be understood in the context of a "thick" topology of the uneven distribution of communications opportunities in the lives of individuals and communities. Topologies can be regarded as theoretical though not necessarily fully representational models (Mäki 2001), of movement and structure that can be mapped or analysed for new relationships, connections, opportunities, limitations, constraints, or boundaries. However, such mapping or modelling is not upon a flat surface, but drawing upon critical theory and information continuum theory (Stillman & Upward 2007), social-technical relationships are strongly constructed through and embedded in the uneven topology created by particular social formations (Stillman & Linger 2009). Sociologically, Giddens argues that a feature of modernity is the disembedding and disruption of traditional ways of thinking and doing, and "the modes of life brought into being by modernity have swept us away from all traditional types of social order, in quite unprecedented fashion" (Giddens 1990, p. 4). Giddens also views this process of change in an essentially positive way, aware of the capacity for personal reinvention and personal innovation.

Furthermore, in the modern era people's "locales" are no longer just physical, but also virtual constructions. "Locale" can no longer be simply associated with physical places where routine and recursive actions take place, but locales also exist through virtual exchange. While physical co-presence has been associated with this activity in the past, it is now clear that meaningful, contextualised exchange also takes place electronically (Giddens 1984, p. 118, Thrift 1996). Furthermore, these locales appear natural and domesticated to users: people are at home in virtual spaces and places.

However, from a Marxist perspective, the unfair distribution of resources in particular time-space constructions is the basis of power in which time- and space are manipulated to produce particular outcomes. Harvey writes: "concepts of space and time and the practices associated with them are far from socially neutral in human affairs" (Harvey 1990, p. 424), and this adds a politically relevant critique to the otherwise important insights of geographers such as Hagerstrand about how daily life is constructed in different ways around the navigation of time and space zones (Hagerstrand 1970, 1975). Movement across time and space is unequal, privileging some groups over others. We can call this *communicative disruption* which acts as a corrective to *communicative optimism*. Thus a person with a car – as a means of communication – can travel a long way to work in a short amount of time, and still have time to visit the gym and go shopping. Yet this should not be theoretically extrapolated as a normative condition, where it is assumed that all have equal access. The reality is that for those left on the margin who do not have private transport, and need to walk or take slow forms of public or semi-public transport, the "compression" of time for communication purposes can be missing and disruption and disjuncture continue. Likewise, the physical and communicative distanciation that is created by new communications systems (such as the mobile phone) creates a new and increasingly complex social and geographic topologies (Upward & Stillman 2007).

The concept of disruptive technologies can also be re-examined. In main-stream thinking, *disruptive technologies* are those which displace current or incumbent technologies or practices to the structuring of distance (time or geographic) and communicative relationships in everyday life. This is over-whelmingly viewed as a positive form of disruption. As an example, while fixed-line telephones were originally dismissed as peripheral and marginal to established technologies and their business interests (telegrams, letters), it in fact revolutionised communications, and in turn, social and economic relations. In time, it was overtaken by the "simple" mobile phone and today mobile phones are being disrupted by other innovations and functionalities, which in turn will be replaced by others functions or devices (Bower & Christensen 1995, Danneels 2004). However, while such disruptive technologies can be positively transformative, there is another perspective which is more critical of unquestioned change. It understands that "technological interventions, like many other forms of development can be highly political and controversial... both as a concept and as an area of policy for international and local action" (Avgerou 2010, p. 6).

Consequently, within ICT for Development thinking, there is a stream critical of a simplistic and deterministic viewpoint that what works for technology innovation in the North sets the paradigm for the development in the South (Avgerou & Walsham 2000). It should be remarked that as well, the same simplistic assumptions about the benefits of technology can ignore the gendered nature of interaction with ICTs and the continuing secondary situation of many women, despite automation and connectivity (Huws 2003), or the historical tendency of technical systems to dominate rather than empower (Feenberg & Friesen 2012). More often than not, when the same sets of economic and social relationships are reproduced in developing countries, inequalities, particularly those associated with gender, tend to prevail and disruption continues to reinforce inequity, rather than capability (Sen 2001). The beneficiaries are metropolitan elites, rather than the communities most on the ground which would benefit from a more equitable distribution of communication resources. What Heeks has called ICT4D 1.0 only served to reinforce dependency and "cookie-cutter" solutions with resultant implementation failures. Even the telecentre movement, so widely touted as a solution for developing countries, faces problems of sustainability and scalability.[3] In contrast, it is hoped that ICT4D 2.0 and "positive disruption" will enable widespread content availability and opportunities for networked forms of business and employment because wireless, rather than copper wires have provided a platform for leapfrogging the lack of conventional infrastructure (Heeks 2009). But even this apparently positive

---

[3]   The most recent example of this is the failed roll-out of telecentres in South Africa. "The Universal Service and Access Agency of SA (USAASA) aimed to rollout more than 280 telecentres since 2006, but to date only managed to achieve just over half of this, even though millions have been spent...Of the 160 established centres so far, only 96 are operational. This is due to, among other reasons, obsolete equipment, centres burnt down during service delivery protests, vandalism, stolen equipment, disintegrated management structures, failure to pay service providers, part of the buildings being used as taverns and incomplete centres." Farzana Razool in IT Web Financial (http://www.itweb.co.za/index.php?option=com_content&view=article&id=58149, 21 August 2012). This report also led to many comments on the ciresearchers listserv (vancouvercommunity.net/lists/info/ciresearchers) reflecting on the endemic problems with such a model in developing countries.

move can be criticised for misconstrued optimism about its real effects, as noted in the introductory remarks to the chapter.

The final type of disruption to be considered is *social disruption*, and this is associated with negative social effects. Social disorganisation theory takes the view that the breakdown of family and community institutions and abiding social connections (such as religion, schools, local government, or informal organisations) rather than material poverty or local ecological conditions, is a key variable in criminalising and marginalising communities and disrupting positive social connection. There are plenty of examples of poor communities where crime rates are low, but social capital is high. This of course does not mean that social organisation does not exist in disrupted communities (for example amongst gangs), but the sense of general connectedness and distributed safety is missing from the community (Jensen 2003). Social disruption can even go a step further, and be associated with social trauma in extreme cases (such as war), or in situations of forced migration. In South Africa, the policy of forced deracination and separation from traditional land-holdings has had massive trans-generational social effects (Van Onselen 1996), that continue in the post-apartheid era. As discussed, shanty towns are a direct result of this deracination and attempt to prevent black people from having permanent homes in urban areas under apartheid under the "pass system" which controlled where people could live (Welsh 2009, p. 58). For those subject to apartheid "the predictability of everyday life is suspended; ordinary time seems to stop... and the social fabric is disrupted. Under the impact of [this] shocking event, feelings of hopelessness, apathy, fear, and disorientation spread in the community" (Giesen 2001, p. 14473).

Zanspruit as a disrupted community

Zandspruit, like many informal settlements or slums, can be considered as a disrupted community in terms of all the types of disruption discussed above. Interviewees and their extended families have all experienced communications, social and physical disruption. I asked participants in the case study about the move from village or a rural area into Zandspruit and the differences between rural and shanty-town life. Sometimes one or more parents had stayed behind. In one case, parents lived on different sides of Johannesburg; such was the difficulty of transportation and the location of work. Some interviewees recounted sitting around the fire at night hearing traditional stories from their grandmothers in the village, but this did not happen in the informal settlement.

Such is the degree of *geographic disruption* that the tracks and lanes do not even have names in the urban shanty town. Houses only have plot numbers, and are often located in warrens. This makes it very difficult for the outsider to easily locate a person without asking strangers for a person or location, and there is no guarantee of success. It was considered virtually impossible for me as a white person to make my way safely through the warren of shacks or even follow directions. A black visitor would have to be met or remember the physical markers described from a text message or phone call. With its lack of serviceable or even marked roads, even the police and ambulance vehicles cannot go into the tiny lanes in the settlement. There is no postal delivery inside the settlement because of the lack of marked roads. Thus, for the majority of people who drive past Zandspruit every day, Zandspruit remains a blur, much like any other shanty town lying on the edge of a highway. It is not a place to go into. Even the supermarket complex next to it is not seen as a safe place.

It is also too dangerous to send a child on his or her own on a short errand. This locational difficulty was made very clear in the interviews I had with the students and, as one person put it to me, "we don't even have addresses". This is a severe form of disruption: despite having a physical place to sleep – a shack – it is not considered an address either by the person who lives there or (and particularly) by the legal authorities. Thus, for all the people from Zandspruit and other poor communities

> If you are trying to get in touch with someone, and you don't know where they live, unless they have a mobile phone it is very hard to find someone.

This may explain why mobile phones are so vital for people without a conventional address – they provide location and connection, even if that location is in fact not physically permanent. You can at least be found and tracked.

The disruption caused by movement away from homelands has already been discussed, but the disruption can also continue in other ways. A person who spends time walking through a muddy settlement or broiling sun to get to the minibus station, then has to wait for a bus, then get a bus and then walk from the bus stop to the mall to work, pick up some food at the road side, and then do the same return journey, cannot be easily considered to have a better sense or condition of wellbeing from working in a low-paid job in the shopping mall next to the bus stop. It still takes hours to get to work for low pay. Additionally, if a student takes two hours to walk 10 kilometres to get to school and back, the capacity for her to learn not just in that day, but on any day can be considerably reduced due to tiredness, lack of adequate nourishment, illness, general emotional stress and any number of other factors. Compare that to a person who has easy access to the shopping mall or private school by car and can listen to the news on the car radio in comfort, in contrast to being squashed into a shared taxi or back of a van.

Even the colour of the day can be a disruption that adds to the difficulty of secure living, taken for granted by more affluent people. Come dusk, the dark is the colour of danger. Movement and activity are restricted by darkness. All the interviewees mentioned the danger of moving around Zandspruit after dark, or of walking from Monash South Africa to Zandspruit in the dark. Even having a mobile phone does not guarantee safety and it may in fact attract a robber if you are seen talking. Interviewees also confirmed with me their fear of gangs in their informal settlements. The cost of transport means that students have to leave campus early to be home before dark and danger arrive, and the following quotation reinforces the restriction offered by not being able to have illumination, even from candles, to do homework. Being forced to live in the dark because of poverty disrupts educational opportunity.

> It would be good to have the extra time. If I leave for home at 5.20 it's 6.15 when I get to Zandspruit. It would be good for a student like me to have that extra time. It's already dark, and we use candles. We have three-room shack. My brother is using a candle for his homework, I have to wait for him, and maybe all the other candles, by the time it's already 9.30 and everyone is sleeping and I'm now the only one trying to work and I have only a very small candle. That's a lot of stress.

The disruption to traditional communication

As already observed, internal migration over many decades has meant that many South Africans, because of geographic disruption, are far from their traditional homes. In decades past, communication was oral, or in writing (if literate), or at least there was someone who could read or write for you. In the old days, phone calls were not that common. People became separated over time and space. Messages and objects were sent through chains of people. In the interviews I conducted, I asked people how they would send a parcel to another person in another town. It was still too difficult and costly to use the post office, and many people did not have fixed addresses as distinct from numbers on shacks that gave no idea of location. The best way of getting a parcel to someone was to give it to a trusted person who could give it directly to the intended recipient or pass it onto another person.

One of the interviewees, older than the others, remembers life in the village before they had phones. These were public phones at the post office, not private phones. People also sent telegrams and they had to be short and straight to the point, lacking much of the nuance and emotion that might otherwise be carried in significant person-to-person communication, resulting in profound emotional stress because of the distancing forced by such restricted forms of communication. They were only used to send important messages, such as a notification that someone had died. It would be easy to get things wrong unless the message was short and clear. Interviewees also talked about their mothers writing letters to other relatives or to a father away in the mines. One mentioned that this would happen on a monthly basis, and another said (and this is so easy to forget today) that, "by writing letters she could talk about things that others didn't know about", even though of course, the time lapse between sending and receiving a reply might be quite long as compared to today's standards, but it is something that is in the experience of anyone who has communicated by mail before the age of the Internet. Letters are asynchronous and while there may be the opportunity to write a long letter, problems with personal literacy – or dictating to another person – probably resulted in a very different form of communication exchange with the recipient for many people in South Africa. The long-term effect might of course be that people stopped communicating and relationships broke down, a familiar migration story.

Another interviewee provided a fascinating account of how traditional family and clan networks exist. He talked about a notebook that was kept at his grandmother's home. In the book were the names and addresses and mobile phone numbers of many family and clan members, and once a month, where possible, they come together. There are perhaps up to 500 people who support other clan members with weddings and funerals. The notebook was, and continues to be, a critical piece of database technology (a list of valuable, manually interrogated information) to make connections between a distributed family networked. The interviewee was not sure if his grandmother wrote in the book, or someone else did, but it was kept up to date. The interviewee was unsure about how family contacted each other in the past, but like the other interviews, we can assume it was through the system of informal networks, passed on information, and in the case of a funeral, telegrams or phone calls. He said that today of course, many people would be contacted by mobile phone and messages passed on. Will a paper-based record of the clan continue into the next generation, or will it be taken up electronically?

Mobile phones and the different forms of disruption

Can we continue to believe that mobile phones offer a way to represent the improvement in people's lives in such circumstances, or are they a form of covering fetish for the horrible reality that structures everyday life? The answer is not black and white. In all the interviews I conducted, the mobile phone was considered as critical to personal wellbeing and provided a sense of identity and a respite from grim reality. On the other hand, contrary to techno-optimism, the phone has to be seen as less than progressive.

Identity construction through the acquisition of things is well-observed in studies of consumerist behaviour, and is of course taken advantage of in product marketing where the newer and fancier is always better (cars, mobile phone clothes). Buying a particular brand or style is an entrée into a fantasy and removal from everyday drudge (Fortunati 2005). Marx remarked that a commodity assumed a social and market value with "metaphysical subtleties and theological niceties" (Marx 1867, Section 4). Others, including Marcuse, consider consumerist behaviour the outcome of the pervasiveness of hegemonic consumerist ideologies resulting in false consciousness that serve to benefit capital and a "false order of facts" (Marcuse 1968, p. 145). This diversion from the pain of reality via a "false order of facts" can act as a diversion from potential action which might otherwise assist people in overthrowing their chains (Kim 2004). In their psychoanalytic interpretation of the technological fetish, Arnold and colleagues also argue that ICTs become not important of themselves through perceived use or status value, but they "are also valued because of the unconscious or unspecified experience of lack, of inadequacy, of emptiness, of disempowerment, and of loss and pain manifest in the ache of unsatisfied desire, and the concomitant desire for adequacy, fulfilment, empowerment and affective satisfaction. To possess, to fondle, to fill, to touch, to use, the fetishised object is to symbolically nullify that experience of lack and its attendant emotions" (Arnold et al. 2006, p. 3). Thus, one interviewee said:

> It's exposing me, exposing me, to get in touch with people every day, because I am on the phone, in touch with people... it makes me feel closer to the people who are further from me.

Now, in situations of such material deprivation as that found amongst the interviewees, is the desire for connectivity and removal from the grim reality of loss and pain a rational desire that changes their lives? Does it truly overcome their physical ghettoisation and isolation from others? Unlike the more privileged situation of middle class people who are surrounded by all sorts of material, manufactured and desired objects (clothes, books, appliances, cars, TVs, DVDs, computers – the list is endless), people in informal settlements have little material wealth. However, possession of a mobile can do very little to change material circumstances quickly, but it certainly helps with the pretence of being someone else and something else, and can provide some emotional satisfaction. Consequently, the following statement made in the interviews needs to be contextualised:

> Most people, regardless of how poor they are, would rather have a phone than food on the table or money to pay school fees – that's one of the negative things. Technology detects me, I don't detect technology. Somehow, technology is invented, somehow we want it because it is invented, not because we want it.

For the very poor, the mobile phone is so important that people may prefer "feeding it" with airtime rather than having food. Of course, if one takes a critical theory view, spending money on the mobile phone is wasteful because it has such a limited capacity to empower and truly change circumstances. Yet from the slum dwellers' point of view, that small amount of connection can be critical, limited as that may be in the context of pervasive disruption. Thus, as we have heard, even if you don't have locatable physical address, you can at least be connected, and this has become a necessary part of the way of life for people.

> You come to Zandspruit even if you don't know how to use a cell phone. The first thing people tell you at their house, is take money, call people, tell them you have arrived in Zandspruit, someone will show you how to call if you don't know how [on a cell phone].

The mobile phone is consequently something more than a discretionary consumerist item for the young people I interviewed. The mobile phone has become "part of a system of ideas, even a way of looking at everyday life. The mobile phone has become part of an idea of the family, of intimacy, emergency and work", even for slum-dwellers (Myerson 2003, p. 244).

Consequently, interviewees felt much more in touch with the world, and able to connect with their family and friends in a way that was far beyond the limitations that they had described as being the case with their parents, limited by lack of literacy, lack of access to phones, lack of transport, with only irregular phone calls and emergency telegrams. In one case, the interviewee had quite an intimate relationship with a white person where they discussed deep personal matters. From what I know of South Africa, this was quite an unusual relationship for the very poor and the middle class to meet in such a way. Otherwise, they were strangers, and were aware that would probably never meet face-to-face, and if they did, there would be an embarrassing silence.

The same interviewee spoke of the great difference connectivity can have in such a deprived situation:

> I was living with mum's sister, she was sick with her daughter, I was looking after her two years ago, we were using public phones – we didn't take her to hospital. My mum left to work, and didn't check if everything was fine and didn't want to disturb. We wanted to make porridge but didn't wake her up – but she had passed away. We had to find a public phone, it was terrible. It is nice now, we can check.

Hearing that story for the first time was gut-wrenching, and I still find it so. "It is nice now, we can check". One wishes that "nice" covered a more profound change in life circumstances though here, in fact, the criticism that I have offered of the diversions offered by mobile phone possession falls way because in such circumstances the mobile phone could have been a life saver. However, possession of a mobile phone should not be used as theoretical substitute to ignore grim social reality. We cannot be personally critical of poor people for wanting to connect like everyone else, though we can approach the issue critically and politically. Thus, we need to keep in mind what one of the interviewees said to me: "I am just like everyone else, Larry, but I am poor". She was conscious of the great impediments to her aspirations and was not afraid to say it.

Concluding remarks

The case study provided a means of looking at the placement of ICTs in society in a different way by examining its relationship to people's lives in particularly trying circumstances. Only through a more critical approach to social order can people's communication choices be understood as an effect of topological disorder and different forms of disruption that play out unequally. Thus, while it is clear that "electronic emotions" are as much at play in the lives of the poor people in the slums (think of the story above about the interviewee's mother dying), they are working in conditions of huge disadvantage and stress. What appears to be positive for the "management and mediation of emotions" – as suggested by Vincent (in this book), and her colleagues (Vincent & Fortunati 2009) – requires a politically-sensitised reorientation to take account of the massive day-to-day challenges in the life of the poor. However, more detailed examination of this problem would also require much more large-scale and longitudinal research.

Does the research presented here consequently offer anything particularly useful for Community, Social or Development Informatics? The key contribution is that it acts as a dampener to determinist and idealistic aspirations that are devoid of social critique and social context but strong on technological enthusiasm. Adams' ethnographic study came up with the idea of extensibility through ICTs. He wrote:

> The dwelling is no longer a solid container: inside and outside, private and public are increasingly brought together by television and other media. Physically the home may approach the ideal of containment, but socially it is a permeable or 'leaky' capsule... constantly coming into contact with the outside world through such media as television, radio, newspapers, books, and computer networks. (Adams 1999, p. 361)

In the case of the slum-dwellers I have interviewed, their shacks are literally metal containers and often leaky and draughty, but their electronic "leaks" are very limited. Because their lives are disrupted in different ways, because they have neither the private space nor the resources to engage with extensible social opportunities, theoretically, the emotional and personal dimensions of connectivity cannot be considered in the same way as studied for the middle class. A new theoretical model for their personal capacity needs to be reconsidered, and this is something that can be addressed through critical theory supplemented by approaches such as the Capability Approach of Amartya Sen, which provides a rich social and material reconsideration of the problem of poverty (Sen 2009).

Thus, is there an easy solution to the problem of poverty that involves a form of social-technical action that results in more opportunity and social justice? Indeed, is it right or proper to engage in what can be seen as bandaid public connectivity solutions when more fundamental social justice considerations need to be taken into account in the unequal Global South? As a suggestion, perhaps a new emphasis needs to be put on a modern version of the old-fashioned robust telephone box that used to be on many corners as a starting point for connective experimentation and community development. Using the Digital Doorway as a model, could robust computer stations or boxes specifically designed for unsupervised public access become pervasive network points for people in poor circumstances, pushing out Internet or blue tooth connectivity for very cheap hand-held devices? Despite only having candles at home, a robust community-managed mesh-network could offer powerful shack-based connectivity to people with mobile devices, and let them collectively agitate. This of course, does not take care of the grand questions of inequality (roads, sewerage, housing), but it could certainly be a focus of a new activity in Community and Development Informatics. And working with communities themselves, other solutions using such strong public hubs for local advocacy could be developed for the difficult circumstances in which such communities exist.

References

Adams, P.C. (1999). A homemaker in the information age. *Urban Geography*, *20*(4), 356–376.

Arnold, M., Gibbs, M., & Shepherd, C. (2006). Domestic ICTs, desire and fetish. *The Fibreculture Journal*, *9*(59). (Online).

Avgerou, C. (2010). Discourses on ICT and development. *Information Technologies & International Development*, *6*(3), 1–18.

Avgerou, C., & Walsham, G. (2000). *Information Technology in Context: Studies from the Perspective of Developing Countries*. Aldershot: Ashgate.

Blackburn, R. (Ed.) (1972). *Ideology in Social Science Readings in Critical Social Theory*. London: Fontana/Collins.

Bohman, J. (2013). Critical theory. In E. N. Zalta (Ed.), *The Stanford Encyclopedia of Philosophy* (Spring 2013 Edition). (Online).

Bourdieu, P. (1990). *In Other Words: Essays towards a Reflexive Sociology*. Cambridge: Polity Press.

Bower, J., & Christensen, C.M. (1995). Disruptive technologies: Catching the wave. *Harvard Business Review*, *73*(1), 4–53.

Charmaz, K. (2005). Grounded theory in the 21st century: Applications for advancing social justice studies. In N.K. Denzin & Y.S. Lincoln (Eds.), *The SAGE Handbook of Qualitative Research* (pp. 509–536). Thousand Oaks: Sage Publications.

Chitiga-Mabugu, M. (2013). The employment effect of economic growth: Introducing the South African economy. In U. Pillay, G. Hagg, F. Nyamnjoh & J.D. Jansen (Eds.), *State of the Nation: South Africa 2012–2013: Addressing Inequality and Poverty* (pp. 169–184). Cape Town: HSRC Press.

Cross, C. (2013). Delivering human settlements as an anti-poverty strategy: Spatial paradigms. In U. Pillay, G. Hagg, F. Nyamnjoh & J.D. Jansen (Eds.), *State of the Nation: South Africa 2012–2013: Addressing Inequality and Poverty* (pp. 239–272). Cape Town: HSRC Press.

Danneels, E. (2004). Disruptive technology reconsidered: A critique and research agenda. *Journal of Product Innovation Management*, *21*(4), 246–258.

Davis, M. (2004). Planet of Slums. *New Left Review*, *26*, 6–34.

Dijst, M. (2009). Time geographic analysis. In R. Kitchin & N. Thrift (Eds.), *The International Encyclopedia of Human Geography* (pp. 266–278). Oxford: Elsevier.

Denison, T., & Stillman, L. (2012). Academic and ethical challenges in participatory models of community research. *Information, Communication and Society, 15*(7), 1037–1054.

Feenberg, A., & Friesen, N. (Eds.). (2012). *(Re)inventing the Internet*. Rotterdam: SensePublishers.

Fortunati, L. (2005). Mobile telephone and the presentation of self. *Computer Supported Cooperative Work, 31*, 203–218.

Geertz, C. (1973). *The Interpretation of Cultures: Selected Essays*. New York: Basic Books.

Giddens, A. (1984). *The Constitution of Society: Outline of the Theory of Structuration*. Berkeley: University of California Press.

Giddens, A. (1990). *The Consequences of Modernity*. Stanford, CA: Stanford University Press.

Giesen. (2001). Social Trauma. In N.J. Smelser & P.B. Baltes (Eds.), *International Encyclopedia of the Social & Behavioral Sciences* (pp. 14473–14476). Oxford: Elsevier Science Ltd.

Gillwald, A. (2010). The poverty of ICT policy, research, and practice in Africa. *Information Technologies and International Development, 6*(Special Edition), 79–88.

Glaser, B.G., & Strauss, A.L. (1967). *The Discovery of Grounded Theory: Strategies for Qualitative Research*. New York: Aldine.

Goffman, E. (1971). *The Presentation of Self in Everyday Life*. Harmondsworth: Penguin.

Gren, M. (2009). Time-geography. In R. Kitchin & N. Thrift (Eds.), *The International Encyclopedia of Human Geography* (pp. 279–284). Oxford: Elsevier.

Gush, K., Cambridge, G., & Smith, R. (2004). The digital doorway: Minimally invasive education in Africa. Paper presented at the ICT in Education Conference, Cape Town.

Habermas, J. (1971). *Knowledge and Human Interests*. Boston: Beacon Press.

Hagerstrand, T. (1970). What about people in regional science? *Papers and Proceedings of the Regional Science Association, 24*, 7–21.

Hagerstrand, T. (1975). Space, time and human conditions. In A. Karlqvist, L. Lundqvist & Snickars, F. (Eds.), *Dynamic Allocation of Urban Space* (pp. 3–14). Westmead, Hans.; Lexington, Mass.: Saxon House: Lexington Books.

Han, C. (2012). South African perspectives on mobile phones: Challenging the optimistic narrative of mobiles for development. *International Journal of Communication, 6*, 2057–2081.

Hardt, M., & Negri, A. (2000). *Empire*. Cambridge, MA; London: Harvard University Press.

Harvey, D. (1990). Between space and time: Reflections on the geographical imagination. *Annals of the Association of American Geographers, 80*(3), 418–434.

Harvey, D. (2000). *Possible Urban Worlds. The Fourth Megacities Lecture*. Amersfoort, The Netherlands: Twynstra Gudde Management Consultants.

Heeks, R. (2009). The ICT4D 2.0 manifesto: Where next for ICTs and international development? *Working Paper Series* (Vol. 42). Manchester: Development Informatics Group, University of Manchester.

Hemson, D., Carter, J., & Karuri-Sebina, C. (2008). Service delivery as a measure of change: State capacity and development. In P. Kagwanja & K. Kondlo (Eds.), *State of the Nation: South Africa 2008* (pp. 151–177). Cape Town: HSRC Press.

Huws, U. (2003). *The Making of a Cybertariat: Virtual Work in a Real World*. New York: Monthly Review Press.

Jensen, G.F. (2003). Social disorganization theory. In R.A. Wright & J.M. Miller (Eds.), *Encyclopedia of Criminology* (pp. 1545–1553). London: Routledge.

Kim, S. (2004). Hegemony and cultural resistance. In N.J. Smelser & P. Baltes (Eds.), *International Encyclopedia of the Social & Behavioral Sciences* (pp. 6645–6650). Oxford: Elsevier Science Ltd.

Mäki, M. (2001). Models, metaphor, narrative, and rhetoric: Philosophical aspects. In N.J. Smelser & P.B. Baltes (Eds.), International *Encyclopedia of the Social & Behavioral Sciences* (pp. 9931–9937). Oxford: Elsevier Science Ltd.

Marais, H. (2011). *South Africa Pushed to the Limit: The Political Economy Of Change.* London: Zed Books.

Marcuse, H. (1968). *One Dimensional Man.* London: Sphere.

Marx, C. (1867). *Capital* Vol. I. (Online).

Mbiti, J.S. (1969). *African Religions & Philosophy.* New York: Praeger.

Mjøset, L. (2001). Theory: Conceptions in the social sciences. In N.J. Smelser & P.B. Baltes (Eds.), *International Encyclopedia of the Social & Behavioral Sciences* (pp. 15641–15647). Oxford: Elsevier Science Ltd.

Myerson, G. (2003). Heidegger, Habermas and the mobile phone. In R. Appignanesi (Ed.), *The End of Everything: Postmodernism and the Vanishing of the Human* (pp. 139–188). Cambridge: Icon.

Ross, F. (2013). Ethnographies of poverty. In U. Pillay, G. Hagg, F. Nyamnjoh & J.D. Jansen (Eds.), *State of the Nation: South Africa 2012–2013: Addressing Inequality and Poverty* (pp. 446–465). Cape Town: HSRC Press.

Schensul, D., & Heller, P. (2011). Legacies, change and transformation in the post-apartheid city: Towards an urban sociological cartography. *International Journal of Urban and Regional Research, 35*(1), 78–100.

Sen, A.K. (2001). *Development as Freedom.* Oxford: Oxford University Press.

Sen, A.K. (2009). *The Idea of Justice.* London: Allen Lane.

Smith, M.L., Spence, R., & Rashid, A.T. (2011). Mobile phones and expanding human capabilities. *Information Technologies & International Development, 7*(3), 77–88.

Spinks, P. (2013, July 31). Protest in the connected society, *The Age.* (Online).

Stake, R. (2005). Qualitative case studies. In N.K. Denzin & Y.S. Lincoln (Eds.), *The SAGE Handbook of Qualitative Research* (pp. 433–466). Thousand Oaks: Sage.

Stillman, L., Herselman, M., Marais, M., Pitse Boshomane, M., Plantinga, P., & Walton, S. (2012). Digital doorway: Social-technical innovation for high-needs communities. *Electronic Journal of Information Systems in Developing Countries, 50*(2), 1–19.

Stillman, L., & Linger, H. (2009). Community informatics and information systems: How can they be better connected? *The Information Society, 25*(4), 1–10.

Upward, F., & Stillman, L. (2007). Community informatics and the information processing continuum. In L. Stillman & G. Johanson (Eds.), *Constructing and Sharing Memory: Community Informatics, Identity and Empowerment* (pp. 300–314). Newcastle, UK: Cambridge Scholars Publishing.

Terreblanche, S. (2009). The developmental state in South Africa: The difficult road ahead. In P. Kagwanja & K. Kondlo (Eds.), *State of the Nation: South Africa 2008* (pp. 107–130). Cape Town: HSRC Press.

Thrift, N. (1996). *Spatial Formations.* London: Sage.

Upward, F., & Stillman, L. (2007). Community informatics and the information processing continuum. In L. Stillman & G. Johanson (Eds.), *Constructing and Sharing Memory: Community Informatics, Identity and Empowerment* (pp. 300–314). Newcastle, UK: Cambridge Scholars Publishing.

Van Onselen, C. (1996). *The Seed is Mine: The Life of Kas Maine, a South African Sharecropper, 1894–1985* (1st ed.). New York: Hill and Wang.

Vincent. J. & Fortunati, L. (2009). (Eds.) *Electronic Emotion: The Mediation of Emotion via Information and Communication Technologies*. Oxford: Peter Lang.

Walsham, G. (2006). Doing interpretive research. *European Journal of Information Systems, 15*, 320–330.

Welsh, D. (2009). *The Rise and Fall of Apartheid*. Charlottesville: University of Virginia Press.

INDEX